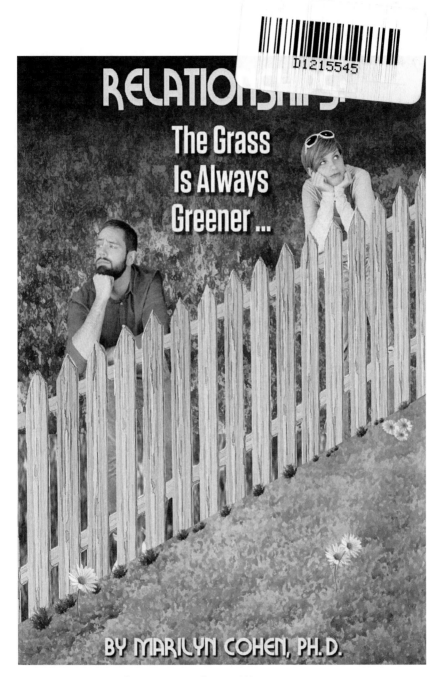

RELATIONSHIPS:
The Grass Is Always Greener ...

BY MARILYN COHEN, PH.D.

COVER ART BY SCOTT WEINBERG

trimarkpress

PUBLISHED BY TRIMARK PRESS, INC., DEERFIELD BEACH, FLORIDA.

LIBRARY OF CONGRESS CATALOGING-IN-PUBLICATION DATA

RELATIONSHIPS: THE GRASS IS ALWAYS GREENER
MARILYN COHEN, PH.D

P. CM.

ISBN: 978-1-943401-44-4
LIBRARY OF CONGRESS CONTROL NUMBER: 2018945726

F18
10 9 8 7 6 5 4 3 2 1
FIRST EDITION
PRINTED AND BOUND IN THE UNITED STATES OF AMERICA

A PUBLICATION OF TRIMARK PRESS, INC.
368 SOUTH MILITARY TRAIL
DEERFIELD BEACH, FL 33442
800.889.0693
WWW.TRIMARKPRESS.COMTA

Acknowledgements

To my clients, friends, and family who have asked me, "Am I in your book?" The answer is, "Yes." And, "No." The stories are all conglomerates of many of you and of the many things that you have shared with me over the years. I can never thank you enough for your trust and friendship – for the part that you have played in my life – and for your participation in this work.

Very special thanks to my three angels, Helene, Carol, and Butch, who suffered through long hours of reading my first draft, offering invaluable ideas and editing that helped me make this much more readable (hopefully!). To Leda, for initially encouraging me by hiring me to write an advice column; to Rob, for his sympathetic perseverance in helping me approach the daunting world of publishing; to Patrick, for helping me sort out the also daunting world of self-publishing; and to Patty, for her artistic encouragement. My special appreciation to David, for his endless kindness and always loving support, and to my other relatives and friends who have always "been there" to listen and to encourage me to never give up!

To my former husband, Frank, who gave me the opportunity to begin the writing of this book in a fairytale house sitting beside a duck pond in the woods in Germany – while he went off to work every day.

And, last but not least, to my Mom, who always put up with me while I worked on this for a very, very long time, and only occasionally asked, "Are you done yet?"

Table of Contents

Introduction   7

Chapter 1:   What's It All About?   11

Chapter 2:   "The Times Have Changed" Hypothesis:
               History of the Single Life   21

Chapter 3:   The Life Cycle   33

Chapter 4:   The Women   41

Chapter 5:   The Men   55

Chapter 6:   The Dating Game   63

Chapter 7:   Choosing "The Right One"   75

Chapter 8:   When You See A Stranger ...   91

Chapter 9:   The Dance Of Relationship   103

Chapter 10:   Love, Sex, And Intimacy   123

Chapter 11:   Commitment   131

Chapter 12:   Roadblocks and Barriers   137

Chapter 13:   Conflict And Sabotage   157

Chapter 14:   To End Or Not To End   169

Chapter 15:   So What's Good About It?   175

Chapter 16:   So What's Wrong With Being Single?   181

Appendix A: The Questionnaire   187

Appendix B: My Research

               1- Summary   201
               2- Recruitment of Participants   203
               3- Variables and Hypotheses   207
               4- Results of the Hypotheses   213
               5- Limitations and Conclusions   227

Appendix C: Quotes and Permissions   233

Appendix D: Bibliography   237

INTRODUCTION

SOMETIMES IT'S HARD to read about something personal, something that makes you wince with recognition, or blush with embarrassment, or drift off into old memories. This might be one of those times, since this book is about the complexities of relationships, especially about being single during the midlife years, something that once was thought to be a terrible fate, almost like the adolescent doom that some of us still remember as "Sweet Sixteen and Never Been Kissed."

Now some of us are single by nature, some prefer serial commitments, and some are relationship addicts. But many still continue the traditional quest to have one special life mate, someone with whom to stand, side-by-side, in the face of life's challenges. Some of us have romantically dreamed of the perfect wedding day or of a gallant proposal, but haven't actually experienced it (yet). Or maybe we have already gotten this far, only to find out that it wasn't really what we were expecting after all. Or perhaps it just didn't last, maybe ending painfully, or even tragically.

And then there are also many, both married and single, who are simply maintaining the status quo — in spite of the fact that we occasionally wonder if the grass might actually be greener elsewhere.

So, if you've longed for love and found it seemed to elude you, or it lasted only too briefly, or it was never quite the "right one," then you can understand the hunger for the mate who will finally find his way past the dragons and through the thorns and climb up the castle wall, or for the lady who enchantingly awaits and will awaken only with the magic of your tender kiss....

Ewwww! Too corny? Well, maybe, but you might be surprised to know how many "midlife crises" are unconsciously driven by the inability to achieve what many grew up to believe was our right: to live happily ever after with the mythical partner who would make everything okay in life.

This book is not based just on social-psychological theory, or on my experience as a psychotherapist, but also on actual research study findings from the past several decades about the numerous aspects of relationships: attraction, flirting, dating, love, intimacy, mate selection – as well as the many complications and misunderstandings and avoidances and fears that accompany having a shared commitment with someone. We'll explore the obstacles that get in the way for some and the differences between those who do seem to find lasting relationships and those who don't. Although the focus is on single men and women during their midlife years, most of the information is applicable to people of all ages, to those who've never been married and to those who find themselves single again, as well as to people in same-sex relationships. Also, for those who might be already happily committed but have ever had any doubts about it (now does that leave out anyone?), well, you might find it interesting, too.

Some of my favorite quotes from other authors are included within the book as well as many anecdotes from my own practice and social network. Yes, you might find yourself in some of the stories, but most of them are a composite of different people (to protect the innocent!). An effort was made to present research findings in an easily readable fashion, generally without giving specific references to the studies. For those readers who are interested in this in more depth, an extensive bibliography is provided at the end of the book, along with detailed information about my own research.

IMPORTANT "SPOILER" ALERT: If you want to take my research questionnaire to look at some of your own relationship issues, it is recommended that you take it first, BEFORE reading the rest of the book, so as not to "contaminate" your responses.

The grass is always greener ...
the neighbor's cherries sweeter ...
the fish are always biting ...
on the other side....

CHAPTER ONE

What's It All About?

**Men and women are infinitely ingenious in their
ability to find new ways of being unhappy together,
so that even with unlimited space it would be
impossible to illustrate every variety of marital misery.**

**L.S. Kubie, 1956,
"Psychoanalysis and marriage,"
p. 15, in Eisenstein (editor),
Neurotic Interaction in Marriage**

WHAT? WAIT A MINUTE. What happened to everlasting love, soul mates, marriages made in heaven? Those words, written by a psychiatrist in the 1950s, came during a time when a change in relationships was just beginning to evolve in our Western culture. Many were dissatisfied with the grim prospect that he described, and so romantic involvements and the whole institution of marriage was going through a major upheaval. Of course, his words didn't apply to everyone's marriage, but a substantially rising number of divorces showed that many of us in western culture were increasingly resistant to the thought of spending our lives enduring such suffering. During the 1960s and 70s this trend kept expanding until more than half of all marriages were ending in divorce. It's still about the same today.

Some accounts attributed this to the growing financial independence of women, or the introduction of reliable birth control methods, or the anti-establishment attitudes of the times, and so on. But, nonetheless, it was only our unwillingness to <u>settle</u> for the "marital misery" that had changed, <u>not</u> the importance that was placed on marriage and intimate relationships. Surveys and studies conducted during this time continued to show that the desire for a committed intimate relationship remained life's highest priority. We still longed for love and romance and consistently listed marriage as the most important part of life satisfaction, far greater in importance than any of the other areas reviewed: satisfaction with work, financial security, family life, friends, leisure activities, community involvement, or even health.

Some research emphasized the importance of having a "significant other" to endure the stressful crises in life. Some studies of the elderly showed that the happiest and healthiest seniors were those who had been married or involved in at least one close relationship during their lifetime. Many theorists said that being motivated to have an intimate and enduring relationship was a sign of psychological health. This was associated with being well adjusted, being successful at work, and with mental health in general. Freud said that the two most important criteria for a healthy life were an ability to work and an ability to love. Existential theorists said that "being" was about meaning something to someone else. Even personality theorists, who focused on the individual, gave particular attention to the individual in relationships.

But these theorists were almost always referring to the more positive side of love relationships, not to the negative aspects of it. We may enjoy companionship, caring, encouragement, support, and appreciation. We may also get to have someone there to care for and advocate for us in old age (hopefully). But, on the other hand, it is also likely that we could get to have the experiences of obligation, aggravation, guilt, coercion, constraint, humiliation, pain....

One woman was complaining bitterly about her husband. He had been a terrible embarrassment to her at a recent family event. He rarely helped her around the house even when she was really sick and needed his assistance. He didn't make much money at his job so she had to take on extra work just to make ends meet. He often seemed to be oblivious to her feelings and was unsympathetic even when she tried to express herself to him. With tears and anger she recounted the many disappointments in their lengthy relationship. So why, I asked, did she continue to put up with him if he was so bad? She thought deeply about my question as if it hadn't ever occurred to her to do anything different. And, in fact, it hadn't. In spite of her complaints, she said she was just "used to him" being around. She felt she wouldn't know how to get along in her life without him being a part of it. (Even a bad part!)

Even with disappointments and disillusionments, we continue to have hope and to long for love. Maybe it was because of the discrepancy between the importance we put on relationships, and the frustration and dissatisfaction we had with them, that interest in relationship therapy and research developed during the 1950s. The field of marriage and family counseling emerged in response to the demand from couples in conflict that wanted to do something about it. There was an explosion of professional and popular books on the subject, marital interventions and relationship enrichment programs, pre-marital counseling, divorce counseling, and a wide variety of other seminars and training workshops. Medications were even developed for improving sexual satisfaction. So far, though, no one has developed a pill that can actually make a relationship work....

Books and articles gave attention not only to marriage but also to single people who were seeking romantic relationships. Researchers and the popular press explored subjects like initial attraction, flirting, dating, the developmental stages of relationships, communication skills, self-disclosure, intimacy, commitment, mate selection, and on and on. However, the focus on singles was almost always on the young (usually college age) single people. Studies and writings that referred to those of us who were older singles, living on our own, assumed that we were just in a brief transition period between living with parents and getting married, or after the death of a spouse, or between a divorce and remarrying. Very little attention was ever given to those who had either remained unmarried into our midlife years or who found ourselves "single again" for more than just a brief period. It was assumed that anyone over 35 who had not yet married would never marry. Either we were opposed to the institution of marriage or we weren't interested in making a commitment, or we weren't heterosexual, or we had some serious problem that prevented us from relating in a meaningful way. If we were widowed or divorced, it was assumed that we would remarry quickly. Those who were continuing to try to develop a relationship with the intention of marrying or remarrying, but who hadn't yet been able to do so, were never really addressed.

Even as recently as the 1990s, references made to the midlife years were almost always about marriage, divorce, parenting, or the "empty nest" syndrome. It wasn't until 1995 (maybe because the Baby Boomer generation was entering midlife) that a landmark study was started about the many different aspects of the middle years – including the issue of being unmarried. This study started with an extensive survey of over 7,000 participants from 25 to 74 years old. A follow-up of this same group seven years later made this the very first time that researchers had focused their attention on the health and well-being of people in midlife over a span of time. A third follow-up of this group in 2011 added some questions about the effects of the financial crisis that had taken place during the previous few years. The mission of all of this research was to try to find out what factors would most likely help the current midlife population to be healthy, with a secure sense of psychological well-being and a strong desire to be socially responsible citizens.

When these findings were compared to the life satisfaction surveys that had been done in the previous several decades, the conclusions were still consistent. In spite of the social and cultural changes that took place during the second half of the twentieth century, The American Story about quality of life still continued to be the same, with the strongest predictor of happiness and satisfaction still being a good quality marriage or a close committed relationship – for both men and women, at all ages and at all levels of education, having positive relationships was consistently selected as the most important aspect of satisfaction in our lives. Once again, this is what produced more of a sense of well-being than any of the other factors that were considered (good health, enjoyment of work, enjoyment of leisure).

Those who were highly educated usually linked their selection with having accomplishments, a purpose in life, and enjoying leisure activities. Those with less education linked it with enjoyment of family, feeling financially secure, and being involved in church or community. But all of us selected relationships first.

One woman in her thirties seemed to have everything she could want in life. She was very intelligent and she had a great job that she loved where she was well compensated and well respected. She was attractive in both looks and personality. She had plenty of friends, both female and male, and she enjoyed spending time with them. She also felt that she could easily communicate openly with them and count on them to "be there" if she needed them. Her close relatives were genuinely supportive of her, seeming to appreciate her for the young woman she had become. She lived in the city in a beautiful condominium and had easy access to many local activities as well as excursions into the countryside. She was healthy, active, positive in spirit, and resilient when she hit life's inevitable bumps in the road. What wasn't she? Married. In spite of all her accomplishments and her ability to enjoy life on a daily basis, she felt something was missing. She was dating a man whom she described as "fun" but who really didn't seem to be "The One." She'd been in relationships like this before — maybe even as her way of avoiding a more serious commitment that she feared might limit her rather than enhance her life. But now that she was admitting to this fear, she was trying to face what was still missing for her. She was ready to figure out what she really wanted in a relationship and then to get out of her own way, her own self-imposed avoidance pattern.

Although all of the groups in the midlife survey wanted committed partnerships, they also listed social relationships as by far their most frequent source of stress! For women, this was usually related to feeling overloaded by a personal network of family and friends, while for men it was more likely to be about problems with co-workers. Men who had high status occupations, and who were either married at the time of the survey or else had never been married (but not including those who were widowed or divorced), were the most likely to have high scores on social well-being. Who scored the lowest on well-being? The least satisfied were women who had lower status occupations and who had previously been married but now were either widowed or divorced.

Overall, the results of these recent surveys concluded that most of us in America view ourselves positively during our midlife years. We see ourselves as healthy, having a purpose, and satisfied with our lives. We're accepting of our obligations to our families and our work, and we feel emotionally supported by our partners and immediate family members. Interestingly, these feelings can be represented in a variety of different ways depending on which region of the country we're from and whether we're living in a city or in a rural area. For example, New Englanders scored the highest on their sense of good physical health and social well-being, as well as good relationships with others. People living in the mountain region scored high on personal growth, satisfaction with their lives, being independent thinkers, and not feeling constrained by others (the "don't fence me in" crowd), while they scored low on feelings of civic obligation or social responsibility. In rural and southern states, it was just the opposite. They scored low on all the aspects of well-being (especially health, self-acceptance, and relationships) except for feelings of social responsibility. On this they had the highest scores, feeling a strong sense of the importance of contributing to the welfare and well-being of others.

These regional differences remind me of a stark contrast between two groups, urban and rural, that I encountered when working in a program that provided Donated Foods for people in need. For example, one couple, with six children who ranged in age from four to eighteen, lived in a farming community way out in the country. They asked for temporary food assistance because the father had a back injury and got laid off, and the mother developed multiple

sclerosis, making it very difficult for her to walk around without assistance. As required by law, I visited them at their home to verify their need. They were living in a four-room house (as neat as a pin) and, in spite of what might seem like dire circumstances to many of us, they all had warm happy smiles and kind twinkling eyes, and they greeted me graciously at the door – all of them at once! It was summer, so the children weren't in school but each had his or her own duties to perform around the house (even the four-year-old) and each took great pride in telling me all about it. The older ones worked in the neighborhood as well, doing yard work or farm work, delivering papers or babysitting. The mother, having just finished cooking one of her specialties, insisted on their "guest" having a taste of it. This family could not have been more appreciative of the help their community was providing to them. They assured me they would soon be back on their feet and they would contribute something in return as soon as they could.

On the other hand, some of my visits to the people living in a nearby big city went more like this one: three people were living in an apartment together while going back to the community college to complete their education. This was an admirable ambition and also made them eligible to apply for the food assistance program. When I arrived at their door for our appointment, I was greeted reluctantly and with lots of questions. "Why do we have to fill out all these forms?" "Why do you have to come here to approve us?" "Since it's donated foods, why don't they just open the warehouse doors and let whoever needs it take what they want?" I tried to explain that if they just threw open their doors, the ones who would get the food might often be the ones who needed it the least. That supplies were limited and the donors wanted to help people who were most in need. That paperwork was needed to keep

track of what was being given. But these students weren't too interested in my explanations. Maybe they were studying Socrates. Always question authority....

Even with an understanding of regional differences and having this new research on people in midlife from all parts of the country, there is still very little that explains why some people do manage to get married (and then stay married) and some people don't. So what about the midlife singles? Will we still be able to find that coveted relationship? Are we somehow different in our personality traits or our backgrounds from our friends who are married? Are we different in any other significant ways from those who married and remained married? Or are we unmarried merely as an accident of fate?

There are some obvious differences between "never-married" midlife singles and those who have been widowed or divorced. Those in the "single again" population were previously able to make a pledge of commitment, but then, after losing a partner, had to deal with the readjustment and the challenges of starting all over. If we are divorced or widowed, we're dealing with issues of loneliness, anger, rejection, broken dreams, loss of a home, loss of friends (since couples tend to exclude those without partners), changes in financial stability, judgments by church or family members, or suddenly being treated differently. We may also be feeling guilty (what else could I have done?), or betrayed (I thought we'd be together forever), or questioning our life (why did this happen to me?). And when there are children involved, the broken family adds still one more, even more heartbreaking, complication.

Never-married singles are dealing with many of the same or similar issues, but in addition, are also often questioning our own self-worth. "Maybe something is terribly wrong with me." "Everyone else seems to find someone except me." "No one has ever really loved me." Does this make the concerns we face in new relationships during midlife different for those of us who have never been married than for those of us who are single again?

Distinguishing among different age groups is also important in answering these questions. Singles in our thirties are in a different part of the "life cycle" than singles in our forties or fifties or sixties. How does this influence the issues that we face? And have we been affected differently by all of the historic and cultural changes that have taken place over the past half-century?

First, we'll explore some of the history and the research studies about the single life, and then examine developmental theories as they relate to midlife, to women, and to men. Then, we'll go on to look at the search for that special mate, with all of its various dimensions, its anticipations and expectations, its trials and tribulations, its excitement and anguish.

Chapter Two

"The Times Have Changed" Hypothesis:
History of the Single Life

During the 18th and 19th centuries, unmarried individuals were generally admired because they were seen as achievers who dedicated their lives to higher causes. Men were in the clergy, or were away on the battlefields, or remained free in order to explore new territories. Women were devoting their lives to teaching, or to adopting orphans, or to causes such as opposing slavery. Then, in the period between 1850 and 1900, a major change took place in Western culture: parent-arranged marriages and marriages based on rational choice started to decline. Instead, romantic love became the primary factor in choosing a marriage partner. Today, this continues across all generations to be seen as the most important criterion for mate selection – in spite of the fact that this practice is believed by many to be a major cause of <u>failure</u> in marital relationships!

As a result of this change, by the early 1900s, negative stereotypes about being single were beginning to develop, especially for women. Single women were being called "spinsters" who didn't have the ability to "catch" a husband. Being an "old maid" was a loss of self-esteem for a woman, causing damage to her family's pride. Being an older bachelor was still generally accepted approvingly as being a "rogue," but it also began to draw suspicion that maybe an unattached man might either be what was then referred to as a "mama's boy" or that he might somehow be socially defective.

The Evolution

Cultural changes continued through the early 1900s, with women gaining in legal rights as well as increasing their earning power, and with overall improvements for women and men in education. Along with these changes there was a decline in customary formal courtship practices. The previously required "parlor" dates, family approval, and being accompanied by a chaperone, were quickly becoming things of the past.

By the 1920s, fraternities and sororities became popular on college campuses. Along with this came something that was described as the Rating and Dating Complex. People rated each other based on their status, money, activities, dress, smoothness of manners, dancing ability, automobile, and popularity. Both men and women would date several people at one time, were looking for "thrills," and were often just exploiting one another rather than seeking a partner for their future. Whether or not this phenomenon was actually as widespread as it was generally thought to be, there was concern about a "new morality" and the loss of meaning in relationships:

Whether we approve or not, courtship practices today allow for a great deal of pure thrill-seeking. Dancing, petting, necking, the automobile, the amusement park, and a whole range of institutions and practices permit or facilitate thrill-seeking behavior. ... According to the old morality, a kiss means something, a declaration of love means something, a number of Sunday evening dates in succession means something, and these meanings are enforced by customary law, while under the new morality such things may mean nothing at all – that is,

they may imply no commitment
of the total personality whatsoever.

W. Waller, 1937,
"The Rating and Dating Complex,"
p. 728, American Sociological Review, 2

What was the actual result of these freedom-seeking changes? Was it a greater sense of openness leading to more romance and more love? Did it increase enjoyment resulting in more personal happiness? Apparently not. Instead, there seemed to be a growing sense of mistrust and antagonism between the sexes along with a growing sense of dissatisfaction in relationships. And these were generally attributed to the decline in traditional courtship practices.

The popularity of the rating and dating phenomenon died down during the 1930s along with the decline of fraternities and sororities, the impact of the Great Depression, and then the sobering effects of World War II. During the 30s and 40s, musicals and biographies filled with romance and sentiment were packing the theatres and covering the movie screens — an idealistic escape from the realities of the times. As described in "That's Entertainment," a film about the shows of those days, the plot was always "Boy meets girl, boy loses girl, boy sings a song and gets girl back."

During and after the war, dating returned again to the more conventional practice of "going steady" rather than dating more than one person at a time, closer to the way it was before the turn of the century. The 40s and 50s then fostered serious values and expectations of life. One was supposed to marry young, live in the suburbs, have two or three children, a dog, and a white picket fence....

Changes in values continued to take place as the war, industrialization, inflation, and an increase in the emphasis on consumer goods resulted in women entering the work force in large numbers for the first time. The domestic role of women, and consequently of men, began to change dramatically.

Then came the wartime babies and the post-war generation that we call the

Baby Boomers. Many of us who are now in midlife were having our values about relationships and family life shaped during this transformational period. Television became available and was soon popularized. It quickly became a source of idealistic programming for our developing young minds. The three or four channels played and replayed romantic films from Hollywood, cartoons focused on villains and heroes, and super-hero stories from Mighty Mouse to Superman. For many, there was a remarkable contrast between how a family was "supposed" to be – Ozzie and Harriet, Father Knows Best, The Donna Reed Show, Leave It To Beaver – and what was actually true in reality. When real life did not resemble these shows, did we think that the shows were fantasies? Or did we think that it was our life that was somehow lacking?

During this era, the status of being single became even more discredited. It was suspect for both men and women. The culture was described at this time as one which:

> **... so values family life that it treats unmarried adults at best as undeveloped, immature, and incomplete – and at worst as failures and willful renegades who cannot or will not take up a respectable and responsible family role. ... Singleness immediately raises questions about one's sense of responsibility and about one's desirability as a tenant, a neighbor, a customer, a friend. The unattached man or woman, after all, may be cagily waiting for a chance to steal one's husband or wife. Common stereotypes see the bachelor as a self-indulgent hedonist, the unmarried woman as either promiscuous or frigid.**

> **George Bach and Ronald Deutsch, 1971,
> Pairing, pp. ix - x**

When researchers surveyed unmarried men and women in the early 1950s, these societal attitudes were reflected in the mostly negative reasons they gave for why they weren't married: hostility toward marriage or the opposite sex, poor health, economic problems, feeling physically unattractive or socially inadequate, unwillingness to assume responsibility, seeing marriage as a threat to career goals, geographic or occupational isolation that limited chances of meeting someone, inability to find "true love," emotional involvement with parents, and some unanticipated life circumstance such as dealing with the death of a fiancé or having to care for a parent or sibling.

The Revolution

I am of that generation that was brought up to believe that women had very special emotional needs, that love was always, or almost always, a more significant or more encompassing experience for a woman than for a man, and that, because of the dichotomies between men and women, it was necessary to protect women against the ravishments of male sexuality. ...
[I was] taught: men respect a woman who can say no; men want to marry virgins ...
don't let your passions (if you have passions) run away with you. ...
By the time I reached the age to apply any of these standards, however, the standards had changed. ...
I cannot be the completely feminine woman of the fifties, the emancipated, sexually free woman of the sixties, and the militant, antisexist woman of the seventies.

Ingrid Bengis, 1972,
Combat in the Erogenous Zone, pp. 197-198, 203

This was the confusion for those of us who were adolescents and young adults in the 60s, when indulgent relationship themes from the 20s and 30s were repeated – or even surpassed. The assassinations of President John F. Kennedy, Martin Luther King, Jr., and Robert Kennedy increased our uncertainty about security and permanence. The crisis in Vietnam, followed by the anti-war movement, and then by the scandalous explosion of the Watergate incident, undermined the very credibility of our government. Traditional institutions came into question and under attack in the business world, in education, and also in marriage. The Women's Movement, the growing availability of birth control pills, and the declining popularity of organized religion, had a radical impact on the nature of relationships and sexual attitudes. The battle between the sexes seemed to intensify … romance seemed to deteriorate … and the divorce rate grew. Many of us, women and men, were confused about how to act: the new concepts that related to "masculine" and "feminine" were developing, but many of us hadn't figured out how we fit into them. We were confused about what to expect. Some new possibilities in relationships heightened our hopes, but our inability to actually achieve these ideals often just furthered despair and disillusionment.

The sense of security that once came from being in a relationship that was both permanent and exclusive became harder to find. Commitments were often made in only a limited way. According to the Census on Marital Status and Living Arrangements, the couples who were deciding to live together without marrying increased by 800% during the 1960s. Some said this was just a new stage in the courtship process. But, for many, it was a new alternative to the dreaded institution of marriage.

One couple had known one another for seven years, had dated for three of them and then lived together for three more when they approached the next decision, with great trepidation, of whether to get married. Wanting to have children was complicating things. They thought certainly they knew each other well enough and they did love to be together. So they decided they should do it. But within six months of "tying the knot," they were starting to have arguments that reminded them of their parents. Each of them had slipped into the

roles that went along with their internal impression of the titles of "husband" and "wife." And they <u>were</u> feeling "tied" in a "knot." He got angry if she didn't have dinner waiting for him when he got home. She got angry if he told her he'd clean the garage but he didn't. He felt angry if she called him at work, expecting him to stop at the store for something on his way home. She felt angry if she wanted to tell him something but she couldn't get him to turn away from reading the news. He was angry if she talked during a football game and didn't wait until the commercial. She was angry if he was unable to understand when something was upsetting her. They had become rooted in exactly what they had feared: the tradition that they knew as "marriage." Before, they were able to easily overlook small things or figure out ways to deal with the issues that bothered them. Now they were stuck. They had to dig out of stereotyped expectations to become once again that couple that they had enjoyed being. They worked to remember how they had managed before, and then to redefine what was really important to them in their partnership. Now they wanted to establish some of their <u>own</u> traditions of what it really meant to be husband and wife.

The Celebration of Singles

Then came the 70s, known as the "Me Decade," with focus on the individual, an emphasis on physical fitness, health food, the growth of the human potential movement, and a return to spirituality. This era was described as a time of self-centered striving for happiness, luxury, and comfort, while the traditional moral, emotional, and social values often lost importance. The emphasis was on personal identity, not couple identity. Our leisure time was filled with activities and television — no need for intimacy. Old courtship practices were long gone and even what we thought of as the traditional "date" seemed to have disappeared. No longer did a man pick up a woman at her home at a particular time, wine and dine her, and return her home again. Instead, singles would congregate in groups, gradually evolving into pairs but staying loyal to the group, usually going places "Dutch treat," and without much structure or protocol.

Society had changed once again, and the status of singles changed along with it. There was a growing culture in which the single life was supported and even celebrated. An article in Newsweek magazine (July 16, 1973) described the opening of a "T.G.I.F" ("Thank Goodness It's Friday") restaurant in New York as a salesman's ploy to meet single women – a thought which rapidly multiplied into a super-abundance of Tiffany-style lamp and fern bars all over the country. This was just one piece of the many singles-only institutions which were becoming part of a newly acceptable American lifestyle, including aparments, cruises, resort weekends, and a variety of singles clubs.

At that time, according to this Newsweek article, a singles' club in New York had 15,000 members; the population of San Francisco was 40% single; within just one year 100,000 singles-only apartments or condominium units were built in the United States; and the 1970 census showed a 93% increase since 1960 in singles living in the suburbs.

When researchers in the 1970s surveyed unmarried men and women, asking their reasons for not being married, this time more positive reasons were given compared to the 1950s list: increased freedom and enjoyment of life; more opportunities to meet new people and develop friendships; a desire for economic independence; and more time for personal development and the search for self-identity.

Not everyone saw it so positively though. Many viewed this as a time of meaningless "scoring" or striking out, a time of loneliness, of sadness, and of emptiness. One owner of a Fridays' singles bar described it as "a place where predatory men prey on neurotic women and where impotent men are preyed upon by castrating females." Some felt that it all became a game of conquest, thinking people were losing the desire or even the ability to move into a more meaningful and communicative commitment or relationship. Meanwhile, others were losing the desire to participate in this game at all, wanting to simply withdraw altogether from the battlefield of meeting others.

Although the negative stereotypes of casual sex and loneliness certainly didn't apply to everyone, they probably – as with most stereotypes – did have some effect on all of us who shared the category of being single. Now research surveys showed some important differences between those of us who were never-married singles and those of us who were finding ourselves "single again." Those previously married described much more unhappiness about the prospect of having to live alone, more depression resulting from being alone, and more sadness about not having anyone to discuss problems with. (Interestingly, this last concern was actually more likely to be expressed by people who <u>were currently married</u> than by those who had <u>never</u> been married). Stereotypes about all singles being "swingers" were not validated. At that time, the great majority of never-married singles reported having had three or fewer sexual partners during our entire lifetime. The number in the single-again group was somewhat larger, but only 11% of our overall single population said we'd had more than ten sexual partners during our lifetime. Of those, 80% were men.

The Party's Over...

When singles were once again surveyed in 1980, most of the reasons given for being unmarried were related to changing societal and sexual attitudes, economic and educational factors that decreased our need for marriage, and an absence of a desire for children. By this time, though, some of the complicated psychological factors were being more openly recognized and expressed: anxiety about commitments or closeness, difficulty with sustaining relationships over a period of time, and pessimistic or negative attitudes about marriage from our own life experiences or observations of our parents' marriage.

With the 1980s came a return once again to more traditional values of conformity and sexual conservatism. There was renewed hope and faith in romance, some thawing of the cold war between the sexes, and a revival of the importance of having committed love and intimacy. Women wanted to find a way to have men in our lives without having to give up the recent gains in our status. Both men and women were finding the previously prized independence and autonomy to be lonely and often filled with economic difficulty as well as emotional regrets. Fulfillment didn't seem to be from career and self-mastery alone, or from love alone, but from both. The celebration of singleness seemed to have run its course. Those of us who enjoyed this status in the 70s were once again faced with being seen by others as either unfulfilled or deviant or both. Even though marriage just for procreation, financial stability, or regular approved sex had become increasingly unnecessary, in the marketplace of life (according to Exchange Theory) if we have not been "chosen," it must be because of our insufficient assets.

In spite of an apparent return to more traditional values during the 1980s, the decades that followed still continued to see substantial changes. In 2009, information gathered from the census data and an American Community Survey showed the marital status for the Baby Boomer generation, including those born from 1946 to 1964. In this age group, <u>one out of every three</u> was unmarried at the time of the survey. Some hadn't ever been married, and about 10% had been widowed, but the great majority were single due to being divorced or separated and then not remarrying. This was a 50% increase since 1980, three decades earlier, when compared to those who were in the same age range at that time. Those of us in this group consistently showed more problems — with finances, health, social vulnerability, and psychological well-being — than did our peers who were married, although the participants who were divorced generally seemed to be better off than those who had never been married or who had been widowed. Those of us who were considered to be the most disadvantaged among women were the ones who had been widowed, while the most disadvantaged among men were those who had never been married. Proportions had changed significantly from earlier surveys. Fewer were widowed but more were divorced, and the number who had never married had increased by 300% during those three decades. Of course, it's always hard to say what is cause and what is effect. Did our disadvantages as singles result from our being unmarried or were they related to the reasons that we were unmarried in the first place?

A different survey (in 2003) of singles who were 40 to 69 years old also showed that most had been divorced, followed by those who had never been married, and then by a small portion who were widowed. There were more single women than men by about three to two. Researchers found that most of those who were surveyed lived alone in single households and participated in most of the same activities as their married peers, although women were likely to spend more time with members of their family of origin. A third were dating someone exclusively, another third were dating but non-exclusively, a fourth still expressed hope in finding someone, but one out of ten (especially the older women) were no longer interested in dating. A small percentage (7% of the men and 3% of the women) had same-sex dating partners. Most participants said they loved having freedom and independence, liked having things their own way and doing things their own way, but that not having a social companion or a sexual partner was a concern to them. Most liked dating in order to have a friend to talk to and to do things with. Only a few singles said they dated because they wanted to find a partnership, or that they wanted someone to take care of them, and a few said that they felt social or family pressure to date. What most wanted was no different than what others had said decades before: we're looking for someone with a pleasing personality, a sense of humor, and with similar interests and values. The women still expressed an interest in financial security while the men still expressed interest in physical attractiveness and in sexual activity. Most were still finding their dating partners at work or through friends and family, but now singles organizations and computer dating websites had far surpassed the church as a place for meeting people.

Historically, in America, it was said that married people had better mental health than singles; but now, with all of the cultural changes and with us living longer, most of us are spending more of our adult years being unmarried than being married. Many aren't getting married at all, those who do are marrying later, many more are getting divorced, and fewer are remarrying. While single men still score lower on psychological well-being than married men, this is not the case for single women. Most score <u>higher</u> than married women on the personality traits associated with psychological well-being. Nonetheless, both men and women still value interpersonal intimacy highly, and believe that probably the best way to have it is through marriage or a committed, romantic, sexual partnership. Some researchers showed that this became even more crucial after the September 11th tragedy, proposing that there was a tendency to return to more traditional ideologies, including the thought that a woman needs a man to protect her and to care for her.

One woman had a close friendship with another for years. They had been roommates in their twenties, had traveled together a few times, and in their thirties had often met in the nearby city to see a show or for dinner or shopping. They both had professional careers and both were very independent in their lives. Then this woman moved away from the area to take a different job and her friend got married, so, although they never lost touch, they hadn't seen each other in quite a few years. When the single one had a chance to return to the area for a visit, she made sure to call her friend and they had a great conversation. Then they talked about meeting and she suggested that maybe they could meet for dinner in the city just like old times. Although she understood that things had certainly changed, she was quite stunned when her friend replied: "My husband doesn't allow me to go into the city alone." Momentarily speechless, her first reaction was that this friend's life had been seriously compromised and maybe she needed to be rescued! But later on she realized that her formerly independent buddy liked the feeling of being protected — even when it might sound like a restriction of her liberty.

CHAPTER THREE

The Life Cycle

IT USED TO BE THAT establishing a committed relationship was associated with the period of young adulthood. Being single was that time when we were just becoming independent from our family of origin but were not in a family of our own. Then we married while we were still young adults and stayed married. Certainly that is no longer the case. Many of us are staying single into our thirties or forties or even later and then marrying. Others are available at all ages in the "single again" category after losing our spouse through death or divorce, including many seniors who are seeking new partners because our life expectancy has now been so greatly extended.

Adolescence into Adulthood

In the 1920s, the average age for beginning to date was sixteen years old – and marriage followed soon after. By the 1960s, the average age for beginning to date had dropped to thirteen, but marriage was coming later and later. What determined this age had nothing to do with becoming mature earlier, either socially or sexually. Instead, it was based on social pressure. Those who began dating earlier were usually from smaller families that were well-educated, well assimilated within the American culture, and were of middle or upper socioeconomic status. So, with dating beginning earlier and marriage coming so much later, the period known as "adolescence" grew longer and longer.

According to developmental theory, each stage in life is related to accomplishing a particular life task. Adolescence is a time for "identity resolution," for discovering who we are. Once the struggle with identity has been resolved, then the next task that must be undertaken in order to make the transition into adulthood is called the "achievement of intimacy." Theorists said if the identity stage didn't get properly resolved, then the possibility of intimacy would be blocked and only superficial or impersonal relationships would be formed. Research supported the idea that we're more likely to develop mature and lasting relationships if we first have a period of time to explore occupational goals or prepare ourselves for a chosen role in life before we make a commitment to marriage. Some of the research also showed that those who had unresolved emotional problems as adolescents (usually depression or anger), were much more likely to have problems in our adult, especially midlife, romantic relationships.

So this transition from adolescence into adulthood requires first discovering our individual identity and then going on to achieve intimacy with a compatible partner. And since developmental theorists considered the accomplishment of intimacy to be getting married, the implication was that <u>single people never fully achieve adulthood</u>.

According to some statistics, even if we continue to be interested in achieving the intimacy task through marriage, the likelihood of actually marrying decreases as we age. Although there isn't any real evidence to support the belief that people tend to become more conservative as they get older, there is some evidence that our ability to change or to adapt does, in fact, decrease with age. In other words, it's much easier to fall in love when we're twenty and still forming our identity than when we're forty and becoming set in our ways! Also, finding a mate in midlife becomes even more difficult for women than it is for men since women usually seek and prefer men in our own age range while men are usually looking to date and marry younger women.

Midlife

The importance of a "midlife" stage of life first began to get a lot of attention in the 1960s and 70s. Just as the stage of adolescence began to emerge historically when children were no longer needed as factory workers or as farm workers, the midlife stage began to emerge as a result of our significant increase in life expectancy. In 1920, a man could expect to live about 54 years and a woman could expect to live about 55 years. By 1980, this probability had dramatically increased to 70 years for men and 77 for women. According to the most recent census in 2010, this has increased still further, to 76 years for men and 81 years for women. Part of this increase is due to averaging because infant mortality rates have continued to drop lower and lower, part of it is due to extraordinary advances in medicine and preventative health care, but nonetheless the average period for a midlife phase of life has now lengthened appreciably.

Historically, the Jewish book of The Talmud presents the age thirty as a time for attaining full strength, forty as the age for understanding, and fifty as the time for giving counsel. Similarly, the writings of Confucius propose age thirty as a time for having our feet planted firmly on the ground, forty as a time for no longer suffering from life's perplexities, and fifty as the age of knowing and understanding the biddings of heaven.

The psychiatrist Carl Jung proposed a more modern formulation of this based on our longer life expectancy. He divided life into two halves at forty, saying the transition period between the first and second half of life would be the time when we would be able to present ourselves with a clearer and fuller identity, when we would be able to pursue our own personal goals and make use of our own inner resources, and when we would be less controlled by the demands of society or by our own personal unconscious needs.

The psychologist Erik Erikson also described a transition period entering midlife. He said that this was a time when we've already had a chance to build our life and realize the fruits of our labors; a time when we then have to face any disparity between what we had dreamed of becoming … and what we actually are....

According to life cycle theories, then, those of us who are not married during our midlife years could be seen as living in an apparent contradiction. Because of our single status, we are still dealing with issues of adolescence, but based on our age, we're in the midlife transition. But developmental theorists at that time didn't really deal with issues of singles who were older. They seemed to assume that people who were in midlife were married. The psychologist Daniel Levinson addressed the issue briefly in his book, <u>The Seasons of a Man's Life</u>, saying that anyone who arrives at the transitional age of thirty without marrying has experienced a gap in life, a "hole" in life's intended structure.

Elliot Jacques, another psychologist, was credited with creating the term "midlife crisis" in 1965. He described midlife as the time when we've reached the top of the "hill" (maybe this was the origin of the expression "over the hill"). It's a time to analyze where we've been, project where we're going, and realize our own mortality as a reality that we must face. By the 1990's, the midlife transition period had been popularized as the time of the midlife crisis. It became everyone's rationale for relationship problems, desire for adventure, anxiety about aging, or doubts about our current life. Most research studies at the time, however, showed that there was actually no real evidence for such a thing as a midlife crisis. As previously mentioned, there was some evidence that those who had problems with depression or anxiety as teenagers might have a similar crisis phase in our forties. However, it was thought that this was probably because of being more prone to crisis rather than that a midlife phenomenon actually happens to many of us. Studies concluded that, while many of us do face new issues during our midlife transition years, they're probably not related to being some particular age, but rather to circumstances that just happen to be changing in our lives.

More recent research in 2008, though, proposed new thinking about the midlife crisis by substantiating the idea that there really <u>are</u> emotional crises during this period. These studies reviewed the lives of two million people in more than eighty countries and showed that depression and unhappiness <u>did</u> seem to be at a peak during midlife. In the United States, the peak was around 40 years of age for women and 50 years for men. In the United Kingdom it was at about 44 years of age for both. This peak was found to be true for all people, whether single or married, whether rich or poor. It was not related to children, divorce, income, job, or any other factors. The researchers didn't discover why it happened, but they were encouraging that our well-being could be just as positive and happy at 70 as at 20 if we remain reasonably healthy and involved.

There were two men in their forties, one married and one single, who were grieving the sudden loss of one of their closest friends. They saw each other at the funeral and decided to get together so they could talk about it over a beer. The married one, noticeably shaken, struggling to hold back his emotions, admitted that he was worried about his own life. He wondered whether he was really happy, whether he had done what he really wanted to do with his life. He grinned when his single friend said that his wife was still beautiful, jokingly suggesting that they change places for a few months. But he was serious that he really thought he wanted a change. His children had gone off to college and his wife seemed so distant these days. And, although he put a lot of effort into his work, his job no longer seemed challenging. After a long night of talking, he made a decision. He tearfully but amicably separated from his wife and moved in with his friend for the time being. Then he started to do some of the things that he thought were missing in his life. He bought a red sports car (what else?) and some stylish new clothes. He went to local bars with his new roommate and eyed all the ladies. He took a weekend motorcycle tour. He bought season tickets for some local football games. He spent time at the gym trying to get into shape – well, also eying the ladies. Then he began to drink a little too much, try out a few popular new drugs, and had a "date" that left him unable to get to work on time the next day. But was he happier? After this went on for a while, his roommate was the one who helped him see that the life he thought he was missing was not really the life for him. It was just a temporary adventure. Following the agreement that he had made with his wife, at the end of six months he called her, asking her out on a date. When he went to pick her up, she really did look beautiful, just as he had remembered from years before. They went to a quiet restaurant and, after a few moments of an awkward silence that had been their habit for many years, he started talking to her as he'd been doing lately with his single roommate. He told her about his fears of getting older, about not knowing how to connect with her any more, about wanting to feel productive and useful at work but instead often feeling at a dead end. Very much to his surprise, she seemed to visibly soften, tears rolling slowly down her cheeks. She thought this sensitive part of him was gone, that he was tired of her and just wanted someone younger, that being the mother of their children was her only role in his life now, that his ambitious, long hours at work were his excuse for getting away from her. They agreed that what they wanted was to build time into their lives for dates like this and for talking openly. She wanted to explore some of the things that they could do together now that the children were grown. He hoped to figure out how to share in household decisions, like how to spend their money and when to entertain their friends and family. They both wanted him to move back home.

Ironically, his single friend also had an awakening from their experience. He realized he was living the free and adventurous life that many of his married friends envied, and, for the most part he really liked it. He had not had some of the family experiences that his friends had, but he took pride in living a purposeful and useful life, being a principled and decent man, and staying a trustworthy and dependable friend. He enjoyed his time alone as well as with other friends, and he loved having a comfortable and welcoming home. On the other hand, he hadn't ruled out finding a partner. Maybe he was ready. He decided he might just call on the widow of the friend who passed away, a woman he had always kind of admired from afar, just in case she might be in need of anything. And, well, you know, just in case....

Some very recent research has shown evidence that if we're in midlife and living alone, we're twice as likely to develop cognitive impairment (dementia), or Alzheimer's disease, as if we're living with someone else. The risk is even greater if we've lived alone during both our midlife and our older years. These results were found to be true for both men and women although with somewhat higher probabilities for men. This is even more pressure for that highly valued pursuit of pairing....

The New Midlife

Now the men and women under 35 seem much less concerned than we used to be with selecting and learning to live with a mate, or with starting their own home and family, even though there continues to be an awareness of the ticking in the background of the "biological clock." Current studies of people in their thirties who haven't yet chosen to settle down no longer show any difference in self-esteem or adjustment from their peers who are married. The percentage of young people postponing marriage increases with higher education, and then some of the well-educated singles adapt successfully to the life of being single and become even less likely to marry.

Those who are older and still expressing the wish to marry, though, will often find less opportunity to meet suitable partners (thus the rise of computer matching services) or will repeatedly find unsuitable or unavailable partners because of some unresolved psychological issue. Some choose to date only casually or to have serial relationships. But many who might still hope to marry continue throughout the midlife years to struggle with unrealized dreams and expectations, to mourn the loss of not having had a family, and eventually to reluctantly have to adjust to a new self-concept.

So, what is it about those who have successfully resolved the basic identity task and work in a satisfying job or profession, but who still haven't been able to resolve the struggle of achieving intimacy through marriage? What about those who managed to build a committed relationship but only temporarily? And is there some reason why this happens to some and not to others?

Chapter Four

The Women

The woman I've continued to be is a contradictory and uncertain human being. Believing in love, I am also terrified of it. Believing in stability, I live a thoroughly unstable life. Believing in marriage, I have never risked it. I am occasionally attracted to men exclusively on the basis of their sexuality, but am appalled when they are attracted to me on the basis of mine. I care about affection and doubt my capacities for it. I fantasize about conducting five love affairs simultaneously while living in sexless seclusion for long periods of time.

Ingrid Bengis, 1972,
<u>Combat in the Erogenous Zone</u>, p. 203

WHEN A WOMAN REMAINED unmarried in the past, she suffered a loss of self-esteem and damage to her family's pride because of her "old maid" status. Society required her to continue to seek a permanent relationship. She was expected to wait until marriage to establish a context for her life, so until then she had no real "identity." Her economic and social power was disproportionate to that of a man, so the cost of being unmarried was much greater for her. Since she hadn't followed the role model that was expected, she was also likely to experience emotional stress or dissonance. Research in the 1950s showed that women who placed career above family were higher in anxiety, depression, and hostility. In spite of the challenges, though, as time went on, more and more women were aspiring to having a career — although preferably a life that combined both family and career.

By the 1970s and 80s, life satisfaction surveys dramatically contradicted the old stereotypes about disappointed spinsters and swinging bachelors. They showed that it was actually the women and not the men who were the more content as singles and, even compared to married women, single women were found to be healthier, less passive, less phobic, and less depressed. But, in spite of this evidence that they were leading full and contented lives, most single women still didn't consider themselves to be complete. They still believed that marriage was the most essential ingredient for fulfillment.

According to the early developmental theorists, a girl was expected to explore an identity while still remaining close to her same sex parent, her mother, so closeness and relationship was already her natural identity. But, as a woman, she still needed a spouse to validate this identity, and finding someone was her pathway to adulthood. Although not marrying might have meant not having achieved adulthood for both men and women, at least men could achieve their identity by pursuing an occupation. For a woman, not marrying implied that she had not even accomplished the basic task of adolescence, that of forming a "legitimate" identity.

Some theorists proposed that maybe this task of identity formation before going on to the intimacy task wasn't necessary for women since their process was so different than it was for men. Because of identifying with her mother, so intimacy and relationship were already her primary focus during adolescence, these theorists thought the crucial issue for women in identity formation might then instead be related to "locus of control." That is, a woman achieved a strong identity if she developed an internal locus of control (thinking that what happens in life is a result of her own actions or efforts) rather than an external one (thinking that what happens is based on luck or fate and is independent of what she actually does or how she behaves). When she can understand and attribute the causes of her successes or failures to her own efforts rather than to a person or an event outside of herself, this promotes her self-confidence and self-esteem.

Also according to these developmental theorists, if a woman marries while she is very young but then loses her spouse through divorce or widowhood during midlife, she probably has to deal with more than just the usual loss issues. Since she will be "single again" during her midlife years, she may also struggle with earlier tasks like identity and dependency that might not have been resolved because she married young. She might be figuring out for the first time how to manage life on her own.

A woman who had been married for nearly forty years lost her husband unexpectedly when he was diagnosed with a terminal illness and then survived for only a brief period. She went quickly through the stages of disbelief and anger, and was able to get to acceptance of his fate enough to have a very loving and sharing ending with him. They spent many hours reminiscing about their lives and talking about some of their feelings, including lost hopes and dreams, deep roots and trust built from knowing one another for so long and essentially growing up together. But it took much longer after he was gone for her to get through the sadness of loss and deal with acceptance of her own fate. She didn't realize how dependent she was on him for so many things. They had no children so they did everything together, they went everywhere together, encouraged each other, argued with each other, laughed with each other, cried with each other. He was the one who was more social, who did the driving, who made the coffee, who changed the

light bulbs and fixed the closet door when it wouldn't close. It was his family that usually got together with them on the holidays. Depression and anger took a lot of her energy at the beginning, but she was grateful for friends and family keeping her company, not abandoning her as she had feared, grieving with her, guiding her. They took her to driving classes until she was feeling safe on her own. They invited her to lunch and dinner until she began to feel confident that people liked her for herself, not just because she had been the wife of her late husband. She took on projects that she hadn't tried before and found that she could actually be successful at many things. The positive steps were also interspersed with some moments of agonizing loneliness, anxious confusion about her fantasies about men and her reactions to men who were attracted to her, brooding over past mistakes, and stewing over what could/should have been. But such moments grew fewer as her sense of independence and self-esteem grew stronger.

More recent testing of these developmental theories show that women and men are actually fairly similar developmentally when they see themselves on similar life paths. Girls as well as boys who have had time to explore occupations are able to achieve the task of identity resolution, and both are better able afterwards to go on to successfully develop mature relationships and commitments. That earlier thinking, though, probably still has an effect on the women who are currently in midlife and who were raised under the conditions that promoted the original theory. It's still very recent that our country has even acknowledged a true occupational identity for women. Although women were already prominently in the work force for decades, it wasn't until 1980 that the census reported the socioeconomic status of a woman separately from that of either her father or her husband.

Most of the studies during the 70s and 80s that addressed occupational issues of women in midlife, showed that both married and single women with careers generally had higher self-esteem and were more satisfied with their lives than non-career women. The women who expressed the most unhappiness were actually those who were married and hadn't had any career at all. Age did seem to be a significant factor, though. Single working women in their twenties were more negative in their feelings about life and also more stressed than single working women in their thirties. It seemed the longer a woman remained single, the better she liked it — or, at least, she adjusted to it. But, while single career women in their thirties were similar in self-esteem and psychological adjustment to married career women at this age, women over forty didn't seem to be as well adjusted. This was attributed to all the social changes that had taken place during that particular era. These women developed their identities during the time of the "feminine mystique," when they were exposed to strong pressures to be married, so they were likely to have experienced more disapproval and isolation from their families and married peers. They might have felt a certain dissonance in their lives because of this, and saw themselves as being somehow abnormal.

One woman told me that she had a long resume of serial jobs and advanced degrees but still was undecided about what she really wanted to do "when she grew up," as she always put it. She worked at a prestigious firm and was making a good salary, but continued to feel as if she was still searching for the "right" path. Something still felt lacking. She went to career counseling, took vocational tests, examined internships that could be available to her if she applied. Nothing seemed quite right. For a long time she resisted the idea, but eventually she reluctantly admitted that the titles that she really was missing were an "M.R.S." and an "M.O.M." Once she accepted that it was okay to want this as well as having a profession (not that she was "selling out"), then she was able to write out a social "resume" for herself and begin to seek a partner who was intrigued by having a career woman in his life.

Another woman had exactly the opposite situation. She was sure she wanted to be a wife and mother and so she continuously tried to meet suitable marriage candidates.

She attended parties, joined clubs, played sports, went to religious activities, tried computer websites. Although she enjoyed much of it, she grimaced about the men who were interested in her when she wasn't interested in them and agonized over the ones that she liked but who didn't return the feeling. Meanwhile, she worked at a job that she thought of as a temporary way to pay the bills – and keep her occupied until she found "Mr. Right" – but it wasn't at all challenging for her and she increasingly felt that her work wasn't really appreciated. It became more and more unsatisfying, sometimes even unbearable. One day she was attending the wedding of a very close friend of hers when the photographer became very ill during the preliminary events. She knew a little about photography and offered to take the camera and try to carry on the work of taking pictures. She was highly motivated by the urgency of the situation, wanting it to be really special for her friend, and by her own innate love of weddings! Much to her surprise, the photos turned out to be quite spectacular, each catching the couple's love, the joy of everyone present, and the beauty of the surroundings. She had truly saved the day for her friend. Meanwhile, perhaps she had also saved herself. She soon started getting calls from other people, asking if she would take photos of their special occasions. She not only loved it but she found that she was excellent at it, and she was able to quit her job to do it full time. (PS: Just in case you were wondering, yes, eventually she trained another photographer – to take pictures for her own wedding.)

In another study from the 70s, single professional women in midlife (two-thirds "never-married" and one-third "single again"), described life satisfaction as: being in good health, not being lonely, living with a female housemate, having casual friends, and being invested in work. Half of the women had concerns about having sexual needs that were or were not being fulfilled while the other half said that this wasn't really important. Only about a fourth of those who didn't have children expressed any regrets about it. One eighth of the group expressed low life satisfaction and twice as many had some concerns about loneliness, but these were the same percentages that you would find in the general population. Overall, these women seemed quite well adjusted, in spite of the fact that some of them faced serious issues of both economic and emotional survival at a time in society when women were still generally taught to define themselves through a husband and children.

Still another study at this time asked never-married career women, in the 35-65 year age range, their "reasons" for not having married. Most said they just drifted into remaining single because of circumstances that they still considered to be unfortunate. Either they hadn't found the "right" person with similar values and high standards and they were unwilling to settle for second best, or they never got over the break-up of one or more unhappy love affairs, even if they now felt grateful the relationships had ended. Only about one fourth of this group of women said that they stayed single "by choice," that they had either never been interested or they felt that it was incompatible with their career. The majority continued to wish for a suitable mate.

The advantages of being single were listed as: freedom, independence, pride, self-respect, time to pursue career goals, time for personal growth and friendship, and privacy. Some respondents said there were no advantages. The disadvantages listed were: no children, less money, lack of companionship or a sexual partner, loneliness, being the sole caretaker of family members, making decisions alone, having to handle maintenance issues alone, being uncomfortable at parties with couples (or not getting invited at all), and dealing with societal attitudes. Some saw no disadvantages.

Although midlife women, both married and single, had the same career values and behaviors as their male peers, they seemed to be living their lives differently. They had and maintained a much broader range of personal relationships as well as professional interests than the men did. In their thirties, they were involved with family, friendships, and career commitments, while at the same time being aware of their own needs, like, for example, their need for roots. Most felt that they had spent the first half of their lives doing what they thought they were "supposed" to do, struggling with the expectations of their parents and of society. Then, in midlife, they confronted their own unresolved issues about children and relationships, but they seemed able to move through this with more harmony and integration than their male peers. By their forties, they were feeling good about themselves, were fully involved in their careers, and saw themselves as the resilient survivors of both the old and the new norms. They described their fifties as the most positive years, feeling better than ever physically and mentally, and also feeling the most difficult years were behind them. The great majority said that the most important source of their self-esteem as well as sense of satisfaction in life came from their career accomplishments.

One other interesting survey during this time period included older professional women, both married and single, who had been identified as "gifted" when they were still children. These women almost always rated income-producing work as highly satisfying. The gifted women who had remained single had some significant distinctions from those who had married (or were previously married). They were better educated, more likely to have developed positive coping mechanisms that helped them adapt to a wide range of things, and more likely to feel that their parents had encouraged their independence, although few actually had a mother who was independent and self-confident or who had herself worked in a profession or career. Interestingly, all of these never-married gifted women had been categorized when they were children as especially liking and being very good at arithmetic, something traditionally considered to be a male talent. Maybe their higher education and better coping skills can be attributed to having more time available and having more necessity to develop their abilities because of being single. But having an early proficiency at arithmetic is more difficult to explain. Perhaps they had a more logical, traditionally masculine, way of thinking?

Another study showed that women who were highly educated were more likely to remain single. If they did marry and were widowed or divorced, they were less likely to remarry than were women with less education. For both women and men, the frequency of not marrying or postponing marriage increases as their level of education increases. But, in 1963, half of the women who had a doctorate were unmarried while only 5% of the men with doctorates were unmarried.

One report that supported this idea was popularized by Newsweek magazine in 1985. Researchers did an extensive study about marriage patterns in the United States and thousands of people were surveyed. Their findings showed that highly educated women were becoming much less likely to marry and that the number who hadn't married was nearly three times what it had been twenty years before. Based on these findings, the researchers concluded that a college-educated white woman who turned 30 without having married had only a 20% chance of still marrying. If she reached 35 unmarried, the likelihood that she would still marry became only 5%, and if she was still single by age 40, the probability that she would eventually marry was only 1.3%! These statistics shocked many midlife women who were interested in marrying in spite of this dismal determination of their chances. Other research followed later that criticized the conclusions of that initial report – but it did create quite a stir!

The study didn't review any similar phenomenon of the likelihood of marriage with respect to educated men. No reliable data was collected about male marriage patterns. However, the census at that time showed more men than women in the "never-married" category of 35-44 year olds (unrelated to level of education), even though less men than women were in the "availability for marriage" category in the same age range. Some of this was attributed to having more males than females that identified as homosexual. For example, among never-married college-educated whites in that age range, as many as 25% of the men and 6% of the women identified as gay or lesbian. With divorced and widowed people included in the "availability" data, the ratio of men again decreases, as there were considerably more divorced and widowed women than men in this age group who hadn't yet remarried: more than two million women compared to only 1.3 million men based on 1983 statistics. Some of this was because more women had been widowed, but most of it was because so many more divorced or widowed men had remarried – but to younger women.

In the 1983 book called The Great American Man Shortage, the author speculates that the post-war baby boom increased both the male and female population, but since men traditionally tend to marry younger women, this left many Baby Boomer age women without same age men available to them for marriage. The 1980 census showed 130 single women to every 100 single men in the 35-

44 year age range. In contrast, in a younger group, 20-30 year olds, there were nearly twice as many unmarried men as there were women. The difference in what was considered "marriageable age" for men compared to that for women, as well as women having a longer life span, left a much greater supply of women available during midlife. This made men more in demand, giving them more power in the courtship arena.

But a numerical shortage wasn't really enough to account for the whole problem. Some people proposed that since women had to compete more for men, they developed themselves more than the men they were meeting. Then they looked for higher quality. They wanted the men to be emotionally mature, able to express their feelings, and able to give and receive emotional support. In the 80s, there wasn't the angry man-hating or woman-hating that was said to exist during the decade before. Instead, people openly acknowledged sadness, disappointment, and even resignation about their relationship difficulties, although often trying to keep a sense of humor about the situation. Rather than angry, single women were more likely feeling isolated, thinking everybody else was busy and out having fun, and blaming themselves for not having met the right man. Many found themselves in midlife still being asked the question "So, why aren't you married?" and answering with the same old comments about how they seem to pick the wrong men, all the while internally questioning their own deficiencies. Many did also admit, however, that they felt grateful that they weren't enmeshed in some of the unhappy relationships that they heard their friends complain about. They felt this would be much worse than being alone.

Another book from 1985, <u>Smart Women, Foolish Choices</u>, proposed that women end up choosing the wrong men because of unrealistic expectations about relationships or because of their conflict between the need to be independent and yet wanting to be taken care of. The authors suggested that women often lack any basic understanding about male psychology. All too often, the more intelligent and sophisticated the woman, the more foolish and self-defeating were the choices she made, not only in her selection of partners but also in how she acted when she was with them:

"If there's one 'rat' in a room full of nice men, I'll find him."

* * *

"All the men I meet are either boring or gay. If I'm lucky enough to meet a man who's interesting, warm, and attentive, sure enough, sooner or later, I find out he's married."

* * *

"I know it's never going to go anywhere and I know he's never going to leave his wife, but he has this kind of power over me. He walks all over me and I just let him."

"My relationships always start out great, but something seems to happen that causes the man to drift away."

Interviews by Cowan and Kinder, 1985, <u>Smart Women, Foolish Choices</u>, pp. 5-6

Maybe "The Search" for the perfect man — The Super Prince — becomes a way for a woman to mask her own passivity in relationships. "Waiting" keeps her from having to face the truth about her real disappointment. Or she might cover up by having a very critical attitude, finding flaws that allow her to think of men as too weak or too inferior to be bothered with. Or maybe "The Search" disguises her need to see herself as a woman who knows exactly what she wants even though she just can't seem to find it, rather than to admit that she really doesn't know how to get it....

Even with all of the unrealistic expectations, all of the cultural changes, the highly increased popularity of living-together, and maybe even a possibility of a man shortage, there were still more people marrying by midlife than had been the case decades before. Between 1890 and 1940, about 15% of men and 11% of women in midlife had never married. This percentage slowly decreased so that by the 1980s only about 9% of men and 6% of women in midlife were in the never-married category. After subtracting people who were not marrying due to religious practices or homosexuality, the remaining group was really a very small percentage of the total population. And, since the number of people who were "single again" had increased significantly because of the much higher divorce rate, this never-married subgroup became only a very small part of the much larger group of midlife singles in the population.

By the 90s, single women in midlife were less likely to be referred to as old maids or spinsters – but they were more likely to be referred to as much worse: "desperate," "leftovers," or "icy workaholics" who were power-obsessed and seeking only money or fame! Ambivalence about the single status continued, although women were more aware of both the positive and negative aspects of it. Married women might not have the same social pressures, but they also didn't have the same freedoms. Single women might still continue to be stigmatized as well as self-blaming, but they also were often glamorized for their status. Many called themselves the "happily un-married" – and the number of never-married women over thirty-five increased fifty percent over ten years, from three million in 1984 to four-and-a-half million a decade later. For many women, however, being divorced was still considered better than never having been married. It gave them some stamp of normalcy.

One survey showed that there didn't seem to be any pattern to explain not being married that could be related to a woman's background. Singles were just as likely to be from nurturing as from abusive parents, from good or bad role models, from privileged or poor circumstances. Most single women surveyed in the 90s expressed surprise at still finding themselves unmarried, but they also said they valued their independent lifestyle. They felt they had an advantage over unmarried men because of being better at making social connections, but they struggled with concerns about finances in retirement since they believed they weren't as well prepared as men were for planning this.

I have always wanted to be a Renaissance woman.
My mother has always wanted me to get married.
She has advised me to learn how to cook.
She has pointed out that rich men are as lovable as
poor men, if not more so.
But I have always wanted to be a Renaissance woman,
And marriage would interfere with my schedule.

Judith Viorst, 1965, <u>The Village Square</u>, p. 17

Chapter Five

The Men

**All across our land, young men are refusing
to grow up. Thousands, maybe even hundreds
of thousands, are moving toward a manhood that
frightens them. In a state of fear, they rush to join
the ranks of the legion of the lost boys. ... [But
they realize that] pirates have no home. They yearn
for a place to call their own. They are consumed
with a wanderlust that forces them on a never-
ending journey to find peace of mind.**

Dan Kiley, 1983, <u>The Peter Pan Syndrome</u>, p. 24

ACCORDING TO DEVELOPMENTAL theorists, during his early adult
years, the romantic love a man feels for his special lady comes from her dedicated
support of <u>his</u> dream, not from a real appreciation of her in her own right. As he
ages, he becomes less concerned with the traditional male roles of dominance and
aggression and more concerned about dependency needs and the importance of
the feeling of belonging. So a man who is still unmarried during his thirties is likely
to be seeking a relationship because he really feels something important is missing
in his life. By this point, he is capable of focusing on his own capacity to love the

other person rather than just on his need to be loved. Some of his uncertainty about himself and some of the disharmonies in his life have already been healed, so love and concern for another can more easily be expressed. Later on during his midlife years, he might once again seek romantic love in order to reaffirm his youth or his potency in life. This is the time that has often been referred to as the midlife crisis or "male menopause."

During the 1960s and 70s, changes in traditional sex role stereotypes were very confusing and frustrating for a lot of men, not so much because they disagreed with the idea of changing the masculine image, but because they just felt ill at ease with it. While young girls had often been encouraged to be comfortable with both their feminine and their masculine traits, young boys had usually been encouraged to show their masculine traits only. Exposing their sensitivity or their feelings left them more vulnerable to being hurt – and that was incompatible with manhood. The choice was to suppress feelings or to be seen as "effeminate," which meant to be weak. Men learned to experience emotion only vicariously, usually through women.

During this transition period, known as the Women's Liberation Movement, there was an expectation of being able to be androgynous (show both masculine and feminine traits) which left a lot of men feeling insecure about what to do or how to act. Many men appeared to be passive because of their uncertainty about their role. Some others took on the opposite appearance, looking self-centered and narcissistic, desperately trying to prove their manhood by being with many different women, while actually being afraid of getting too close to any of them. Many men felt:

... a sense of being unlovable, demeaned, and betrayed. Some men claim that the women's movement is destroying the very cornerstone of men's sexual identity, is responsible for unleashing anxiety, envy of women, dread, hostility, and exhaustion, and is the main cause of the increase in divorce, separation, and wife battering.

K. S. Pope, 1980, On Love and Loving, p. 77

Some pretended to be happy about these more "liberated" times, but really were not. Their friendships and relationships <u>looked</u> lasting but actually were often brief and shallow. They might party, drink, be promiscuous, act reckless – but <u>feel</u> despair. A lot of men covered self-doubt with false confidence, pretending to feel loved while really feeling isolated.

> **They are bored with women trained into**
> **the more traditional, passive, dependent**
> **mold, but so committed to the conquest**
> **of the women they find more interesting**
> **that they cannot open up enough**
> **to make real contact with them.**
> **They are unwilling to commit themselves**
> **to anyone they can't control.**

M. F. Fasteau, 1975, <u>The Male Machine</u>, p. 72

According to the "man shortage" theory at that time, women were supposed to marry "up" with respect to education, status, income, and accomplishment. This meant that men at the bottom of these categories might find themselves with no one to marry. If this were actually the case, then never-married men would be those at the bottom of the barrel on these issues while never-married women would be the cream of the crop. But it wasn't so.

Many of the women thought:

> **"The men, meanwhile, are spoiled by the**
> **surplus of good women. There's no**
> **pressure on them to try as hard, and they**
> **can get away without working to**
> **improve themselves, and even without**
> **being sensitive to other people. They**
> **get used to being pampered and adored,**
> **even if they aren't all that terrific."**

Interview by William Novak, 1983,
<u>The Great American Man Shortage</u>, p. 16

The single men, of course, saw this quite differently. Many felt that women had impossible expectations and no matter what they did, it wouldn't be right or it wouldn't be enough. They were expected to be emotionally open and emotionally generous, to have self-confidence and look self-assured, to respect women, to have integrity, to be able to laugh easily, and to look attractive. Even beyond this, they were still supposed to be able to change and to grow to please their partner. Meanwhile, the men believed, single women seemed to have become much more selfish and egocentric, overly eager, and hopelessly materialistic. They felt women looked at them as "success objects." The men complained that women were keeping work schedules that left no time for a social life, and that they were overly critical and judgmental about everything — especially men. On top of all of this, they thought women were being hypocritical. They would <u>say</u> that they wanted men to be sensitive and vulnerable, but, when they were, women didn't like it and looked down on them. What women really wanted deep down, men thought, must be the old-fashioned macho male.

Many thought, as the saying goes, "Women, can't live with 'em, can't live without 'em." Or, as it was paraphrased in a Clint Eastwood movie, "Women, can't live with 'em, can't kill 'em!" Fortunately, we can still laugh as the battle between the sexes continues.

One man went to visit his girlfriend, knocked on her door as he had done many times over the past several months that they had been dating, and she opened it — and then burst into tears! He stood there, completely astonished, knowing of nothing that might have prompted this. When he finally was able to get her to explain, she said they'd been dating for quite a while and he'd never brought her flowers. Well, he thought to himself (wise enough not to say it out loud), this had never been his usual repertoire of behavior. And he saw her as an independent woman who might find this frivolous or even offensive. However, he was happy to try to please her, so the following week, when he knocked on her door, he was holding a beautiful bouquet of flowers. She opened the door, looked at him and smiled broadly — and then burst into tears! Now

he was completely confused. He sat her down to talk about it, again, and she was finally able to tell him, still tearful, "You only brought them because I told you to." He was, understandably, hesitant about what to say next. But he was able to convince her that what was important was not whether he had thought of it by himself but that once he knew what she liked, he was happy to do it to please her. That was what showed his caring for her. And that _was_ what she really wanted.

In spite of all the confusion and often professed resistance to marriage, research surveys on life satisfaction in the 1970s showed men to be less content than women with being single. Midlife men who were married were found to be healthier than single men. They expressed happiness more, were less depressed and less passive, showed fewer symptoms of stress (nervousness, nervous breakdown, trembling hands, nightmares, or insomnia), and had fewer mental health issues. Married men also had lower crime rates, higher incomes, lived longer, had fewer suicides, and took better care of themselves in general. Twenty years later, in the 90s, a survey showed this continued to consistently be the case for men (while for women, the opposite was found to be true).

Researchers also found that single men who were in the earlier part of midlife had a better sense of well-being if they had a strong positive relationship with their mother, a sibling, or another close relative. Later on in midlife, well-being was still linked to family connections, but loneliness was linked to this also – being around relatives became even more important to the single men as they got older, but it could also displace their need for other relationships, sometimes leaving them feeling even more lonely.

Maybe an explanation can again be taken from developmental theory. Theorists said that boys had to separate from their mother and learn to identify with their father, so their natural focus was about separation and autonomy. But, once they experienced their individuality and formed their identity through an occupation, they were left feeling their separateness, feeling that something was missing. If they didn't then find someone to share their new status in life with them, they felt isolated and incomplete.

A recent study (2009) showed men in midlife having a much higher rate of both marriage and remarriage, and many more sexual partners, compared with midlife women. The ratio is already in their favor since there are many more midlife women available, and since men tend to prefer younger women, the selection becomes even more favorable to them. In addition, midlife men were also found to be much more likely than midlife women to be open to accepting socio-cultural differences in a mate, including race, religion, and financial status, even further opening up the available choices for them.

The theorists say that if a man marries but then gets divorced or widowed during his midlife years, he is likely to be afraid that his life will become unbalanced, so he feels a strong need to get involved with someone new right away. That is, if he hasn't <u>already</u> done so, even before he's separated or while his wife is terminally ill. Some people may look at this as scandalous, but these men often feel desperate to keep balance in their life and being able to replace their wife is the only way they can see to do this. For other men, though, facing this traumatic change leaves them feeling just the opposite. They're extremely cautious, reluctant to even consider remarrying – or even dating – at all.

A man had just celebrated his tenth anniversary with his wife. They had a big party that they'd planned together, and he surprised her with some beautiful jewelry that she had once admired in a store's window display. She was truly completely surprised and delighted, and the whole evening seemed to be a wonderful event for all who were there.

However ... just two weeks later she sat him down and quietly informed him that she'd been having an affair for nearly a year and that she wanted a divorce. He was completely stunned. He simply couldn't believe it. First, he couldn't imagine that she could have been carrying on an affair without him knowing about it, and second, he couldn't understand how she could have gone ahead with having their anniversary party knowing what was about to happen. At first he was too brokenhearted to be angry. Later he was too

outraged to be hurt. He could barely even speak about it.

Several weeks later, he reported he had suddenly fallen madly in love with someone else and he was considering whether they should move in together while he awaited his divorce. He was elated about it and anxious to immediately make a decision. Fortunately, he was willing to slow down a bit and saw that he was trying to replace what devastated him only a few weeks before. After a few more weeks he realized that his new girlfriend (who was the very opposite of his wife in many ways) was not really what he wanted at all. She was a "transitional" relationship. He understood that he really had to focus on his own life for a while, getting things back in balance for himself until he could see more clearly. Then he'd be able to trust himself to cautiously choose the next step.

CHAPTER SIX

The Dating Game

**For every woman who as a girl spent
hours by the phone waiting for some
boy to call, there is a man who as a boy
could not force his shaking fingers
to dial the phone.**

**Cowan and Kinder, 1985,
Smart Women, Foolish Choices, p. 220**

DATING DOESN'T EVER SEEM to get easy, no matter how many times or for how many years we do it. In the old tradition, men were the ones who initiated dates and paid for them and women were supposed to reciprocate with physical affection. Men wanted sex and women wanted love. Based on Exchange Theory, the more money a man spent, the more affection and intimacy he might expect to receive. The female became obligated to be at least somewhat intimate if she wanted to promote his love and make a relationship with her rewarding for him. An equitable exchange. Traditional women as well as women who considered themselves feminists tended to agree about this perception of a man's expectations, and both groups also admitted to having fulfilled this obligation at times – even against their own wishes or judgment.

By the 1980s, this old concept seemed, at least on the surface, to have changed. Although women were still more likely to be looking for affection and relationship, they had also become more sexually oriented, and men had become more likely to approach dating with both a sexual and an affection-seeking orientation. In addition, women were more likely to initiate as well as to pay for dates.

Were these shifts helpful? There's a big difference between thinking about the concept of equality and actually carrying out the behaviors that are involved, as well as whether those behaviors are, really, the desired result. Many women felt that they had gained more control and less feeling of obligation in dating, while others felt that they now not only had to offer affection and sex but they also had to make the initial moves and pay their own way. Many men, meanwhile, said that they liked the idea of sharing the discomfort of having to initiate dates, that they liked sharing the financial burden of having to pay for them, and that they liked having women interested in them for sex. In spite of what they verbally expressed, though, research showed that many men actually felt more inadequate, more passive, and more pressured to "perform" sexually — even against their own wishes or judgment.

Research also showed that dates initiated by women were much less likely to lead to lasting relationships, especially if the woman was the one who initiated further dates. They were more likely to have long-term success when the woman only encouraged but didn't intimidate the man during the early stages of relationship pursuit; when they kept their own initiating subtle: smiling at the man, making brief eye contact with him, or doing some form of the old-fashioned "dropping a handkerchief" kind of signal. This delicate type of communication seemed to be very important. Whether consciously or not, a man looked for and responded to this subtle encouragement from a woman, but he still really wanted to think of himself as the "hunter."

Strategies

One unfortunate difficulty in the dating game is that public meeting places (such as clubs, dances, parties, or events) tend to promote an "approach-avoidance" type of interaction. That is, when we're trying to be open to meeting someone attractive while at the same time protecting ourselves from rejection. We want to have maximum exposure but with minimum risk. As a way of feeling safe from rejection or ridicule, we use some method of social maneuvering or superficial chatting that we might think is clever but can also seem cruel, and often can actually be self-defeating. Rather than taking the risk of making eye contact with someone attractive, we look past one another, concentrate our gaze elsewhere, or find something else to occupy our attention. Or perhaps we protect ourselves by being the first to end a conversation, either because we're afraid the other might end it or because we're afraid the cost of being polite might be to end up feeling "trapped." So, there is a casual brush-off ("I have to go to the restroom" or "I'm going to get a drink") instead of simply being able to be appreciative and thank the person for the dance or for the nice conversation.

A man said he had learned from his very passive parents to try to avoid conflict at all costs, even to the point of not wanting to meet new people at all because he might hurt their feelings if he wasn't really interested in them. He felt he only had two choices: he would have to follow up with _anyone_ who showed interest in him (perhaps then feeling stuck) or he had to keep from meeting people at all. It seemed to him that if he talked to someone and the conversation had an awkward ending, it always managed to follow him. He would run into the person on the street or at some event and he would begin to feel embarrassed and awkward all over again.

He had to learn two things. First, to be able to kindly and genuinely thank a person for a conversation and move on to talk with someone else when he wanted to. Second, to have the confidence that he would be able to handle the inevitable conflict in a relationship once he had established it. He already knew that avoiding it didn't make it go away – it just came out later in some uncomfortable way. He wanted to learn to communicate openly but with tact. It doesn't help to say, "Well, I'll be honest with you," or "I'm telling you this because I care about you," followed by a sharp blow to the other person's self-esteem. But,

it also doesn't help to be passive like his parents were, avoiding genuine closeness by pretending everything was always "fine."

The approach-avoidance strategies often lead to feelings of failure, making us doubt our attractiveness, or wonder why we always attract "that type" (whatever it may be). It can also leave us focusing on the most superficial qualities of any potential new partner. The strategy itself can destroy any possibility of getting a positive outcome: the desired partner instead becomes our opponent and the goal becomes a conflicting one instead of a cooperative one, a competition rather than a combined effort at being able to connect.

Another familiar strategy is "playing hard-to-get," based on the assumption that an unavailable partner is more desirable than an eager partner. Actually, studies have shown that <u>selectively</u> hard-to-get partners (those we know are not available to others but who still show an interest in us) are likely to be preferred over either hard-to-get or easy-to-get partners. When we know that someone is making her or himself available to us because they think that <u>we</u> are worthy of their interest — that's the key. As pursuers, that makes us feel special. Also, being moderately available to some particular pursuer seems to be more attractive than being either very available or very unavailable. This is the idea that the "hunter" is allowed to pursue and conquer slowly, without feeling either pressured (by too much response) or discouraged (by too little response). Based on the theory of "intermittent reinforcement" from Behavior Modification, this uncertainty will keep us working harder. In experimental psychology, when the mouse makes his way through a complicated maze and sometimes he finds cheese at the end and sometimes he doesn't, he'll be more interested in continuing to try to conquer that maze than when he finds it every time or when he almost never finds it. . . .

There are many positive strategies that are helpful in initiating a relationship. We can let the other person know that we think highly of them, we can express agreement with them, we can emphasize things that we have in common, we can do favors for them, and directly or indirectly (but subtly!) we can let them know some of our own attractive characteristics. Whether or not a strategy will be effective depends partly on how well it is carried out, but it can also differ depending on the personality as well as the relative status of the other person (Exchange Theory again). Of course, any strategy could backfire, losing the potential partner ... and, perhaps, all too often, our self-esteem.

> **One man thought it was really perfectly okay to be late. He felt that it made him seem more important because he was so very busy all the time. One day this man was on his way to pick up his girlfriend so she could accompany him to a very important business event. He had prepared her in advance with how she should dress, who would be there that she should try to talk to, what his intended goal was, and even how long they would probably stay at the event. So she was all dressed up and waiting for him, wanting to support him, mentally ready to play her part in the "show." Meanwhile he decided that he needed to finish up some phone calls before leaving his office (this was before cell phones) and he ended up being over an hour late to pick her up. Apparently <u>she</u> didn't think this made him seem so important. She must have had enough of this behavior already, because by the time he arrived at their meeting place, she was no longer waiting....**

This kind of "strategy" doesn't really fly in relationships or most businesses either. It might happen occasionally in an emergency, but whether we say "the bus was late" or "the dog ate my homework," the responsibility for the outcome still falls on us. This is a passive and sometimes even a passive-aggressive way of dealing with things. It's similar to overeating or not eating, to abusing alcohol or drugs, or to raising some new information or dropping a provocative idea when we know the other person doesn't have the time to talk about it.

Looking for Love in All the Wrong Places

> **A woman was congratulating one of her colleagues on her engagement, expressing how happy she was for her, and saying how lucky she was to have found such a**

wonderful man to marry. The newly engaged woman grinned a thank you and then glanced at her and wisely replied, "You just wait and your man will be coming along soon, too." "Well, I don't know," the first woman said, "I've been waiting for a long time already." Her colleague, thoughtfully looking at her, quietly then said, "Maybe you've been waiting in the wrong place...."

A Sufi fable comes to mind about a man who is searching for his keys under the street lamp one night and someone comes along to help, asking him if this was where he was when he lost them. "No," says the man and points over toward a dark field nearby. The stranger looks puzzled and asks, "Well, then, why are you searching for them here under the street lamp?" The man replies, "Because the light is better over here."

Where to wait or where to search can be complicated by many different things: our romantic ideas about how it's "supposed" to happen, our internal checklists about what the "right one" should be like, and sometimes our wish for it just to be easy ... to only have to look under the street lamp. Those searching for a "perfect" mate or for an instant match might be self-defeating from the start. Often people who make the best partners are not the ones who survive the test of the first few minutes of an interaction. Some of the most interesting, sincere, and sensitive people don't always make good first impressions, but offer great possibilities if they are accepted and allowed to open up at their own pace. Sometimes someone who's quiet or not very outgoing is seen as weak or lacking confidence, or someone who's talkative and outgoing seems overly aggressive or overwhelming. Actually, either one of them could be exciting and inspiring to be with as well as comfortable and calm as a partner. Sometimes it just takes time.

Searching in the right geographical territory might sometimes make a difference. Women usually outnumber men in big cities such as Atlanta, Los Angeles, New York, San Francisco, and Washington, DC. In some states, such as Alaska, Nevada, Rhode Island, and Texas, there are much higher male-to-female ratios. Short of moving, though, there are some other important issues related to location.

According to research, the main settings where we develop important and lasting relationships are what might be expected: at school, at work, and in organized ongoing groups, including religious and political ones. This is because frequent and continuing exposure allows us to get to know one another beyond the initial attraction factors, and this usually results in more harmonious matches over the long term. In addition to these places, "matchmaking" has been an undying pastime and trade, whether by professional matchmakers, go-betweens (for arranged marriages), themed community events, or by our own family and friends.

... matchmaking is actually so formidable and complex an assignment that it has occupied all of God's time since creation.

William Novak, 1983,
The Great American Man Shortage, p. 7

Then, more recently, newspaper and magazine ads became a popular meeting place. There were often more "personal" ads than everything else put together in the classified advertising. Based once again on Exchange Theory, or on the concept of bargaining, the strategy people use to present themselves is one of emphasizing socially desirable characteristics while minimizing negative ones. Typically, traditional sex role expectations are seen. Physical attractiveness is what women tend to describe and what appeals to most men; having status and financial security is what men usually claim and what most women are seeking. Needless to say, it's necessary to proceed with caution in responding to these ads, especially since the line between the conventional personal ads and the less conventional ads (of all varieties) can become very blurred.

Next came computer dating services.   The earliest form of computer matching was originally thought to be advantageous because it would select for people's harmonious characteristics with only a minimum of influence of physical appearance and superficial traits, and with less fear of rejection than there is in a chance face-to-face meeting. The early research results, though, showed that there was only one factor that was likely to motivate people to try more than one date beyond the first meeting: physical attraction. Having compatible personality characteristics or similarity of attitudes and beliefs were not as successful in matching people as similarity in physical beauty (and also if the man was taller and older than the woman). Maybe that's why video dating soon followed as the next popularly marketed product, along with "speed-dating," which might defy any principle other than immediate physical attraction!

Importantly, though, there was one other factor that was found to be successful in the early versions of computer matching, something that is otherwise very complicated to figure out in dating. That factor is having complementary role expectations. This is when people have compatible ideas about what part or role each is expected to play in the relationship. This is something that is rarely discussed and isn't usually consciously recognized in the early phases of dating.

Again, caution is essential when making dates on the computer. No matter how nice they seem in writing, these people have not been introduced by someone we know. They are still strangers. In spite of all of its possible pitfalls, though, this way of meeting potential partners has become more and more popular. A 2010 survey of heterosexual couples found that 22% of them met online.

The original computer dating experiment began as a questionnaire printed out on paper. It was developed, distributed, collected, and calculated by a group of students in Boston in the 1960s, when we didn't have our own personal computers. Now, fifty years later, the availability of this service has expanded along with the availability of computers. Today dating information is easily distributed, collected, and calculated, all through technology.

Again, we need to be aware. Behind the scenes there are many researchers who are also examining and interpreting the information that we are providing willingly online (usually without having any idea what else it's being used for). They're exploring such things as which characteristics seem to actually influence our selection of someone for a date, including things such as age, height, weight, race, income, appearance, political leanings, hobbies, and even favorite brands. Researchers believe that online daters are more candid in the responses they give than were many of the former research subjects, since people were often influenced by the very fact of participating in the earlier dating research.

In many cases the information that is being gathered is being used for marketing purposes, but it's also being used to offer helpful information for singles. Websites and blogs have sprung up that focus specifically on midlife singles, offering dating resources and support materials (e.g., www.midlife.com, www.midlifebachelor.com, www.50ish.com, www.amidlifecrisis.co.uk, and www.midlifebloggers.com). Also, in 1982 a board game was produced called "Midlife Crisis" where the objective was to get through the game having more money, less stress, and fewer divorce points than any of the other players – or else a player could declare a midlife crisis, in which case they had to get divorced, go broke, and "crack up" before any of the other players beat them to the end of the board!

Some websites give tips based on the data that has been covertly collected. For example, one said that men get more responses when they use a picture where they are not smiling or are looking away slightly, while women get more responses when they flirt or smile directly into the camera. Another tip says that women think a man making a lot of money is enough compensation for his being short, but men think there is no amount of money that will compensate for a woman being heavy. Men will tend to rate women's attractiveness on a curve, with most being seen as average, but will usually only write to someone who is in the upper third of their ratings. Women will tend to be pickier, rating most men as below average in looks, but they are still willing to write to them if they have other attractive features.

Although participants tend to be candid in their answers to questions in a lot of respects, it is also true that lying in giving data is not at all uncommon. It's not a surprise that many men will add two inches to their height and 20% to their salary while women will understate their age and their weight. Not showing a facial photo didn't seem to have an effect on the number of responses people received, but certain errors were considered fatal, such as poor grammar, using texting shortcuts, or using physical compliments like "beautiful" or "sexy" rather than more appealing ones like "awesome" or "fascinating." Being a smoker sometimes increased the popularity of women (maybe being associated with being more promiscuous) but decreased it for men. Men initiate about 75% of the messages that are sent, still reflecting traditional roles, with men being the pursuers and women being selectively receptive. Quick responses are more likely to get a follow-up reply. Judgments that have been made before meeting someone don't seem to predict whether dating will follow, but most people seem to like someone less after they actually meet them and the mental fantasy factor is no longer there.

So, does all of this help us in assessing our "market value"? Or is it just another incentive for making presentations and choices that are really only superficial? Can we find our soul mate if the "chemistry" and other indefinable qualities are missing from an electronic meeting? Computer dating has become a very big industry with an increasing number of website markets and participants – and with many success stories – but, like everything, it's probably not meant for everyone. And, of course, even with high tech assistance, there are still no guarantees.

Some believe that the search for a mate can best be accomplished similarly to doing a search for employment. First you have to do an honest self-assessment about what you have to offer and what you really want. Next you need a realistic understanding of what is actually available to you in the "marketplace." Then you are ready to start searching and interviewing. This method is based on the idea that finding a mate takes the same initiative as finding a job. It's not about waiting for a chance happening to romantically appear, but about creating opportunities and actively designing situations that increase the possibility of meeting your special someone.

When you do see someone and you communicate your interest in them, hopefully they will be flattered by your attention, but be prepared, because some people (even if they might be interested and even if you are being subtle) may feel threatened and pull back. Be aware of their retreat signals so you can pull back, too. Continuing to press forward right away can seem overeager, or desperate, and can just be more threatening. Also, the elusive but desired "chemistry" doesn't always "happen" magically, but it can actually be created. Showing your genuine liking and caring for someone communicates your interest, warmth, and acceptance – and then the "sparks" can follow later. It has been said, "don't just be interesting, be interested." And, just as with a search for a job, confidence will increase with experience and social interactions will get easier each time. Practice, practice, practice!

A seminar offered in a large university was advertised as "Increasing Your Happiness." No one knew exactly

what it was going to be about, but many students, professors, and people from the town showed up thinking this was a hot topic. The seminar went on all day but a summary of the information can be given in one sentence. Basically, the teacher said that we should figure out what makes us happy and then do more of it, and figure out what makes us unhappy and then do less of it. ??? That was it? This certainly might not actually be as easy as it sounds, but it does seem true. It's something that we don't consciously analyze very much, but knowing it about ourselves is a good prerequisite for finding a mate to share our life with – and for having a stimulating and satisfying life, with or without a mate.

Still other people say searching for a mate isn't necessarily about making more of an effort, but maybe about making less effort, doing less of what might be preventing us from developing a relationship. It might mean figuring out what hasn't been working and then not doing it, and paying more attention to doing what does work. Or it might mean not searching for what "could be" but making what we want out of what we find. Or it could be simply recognizing what we actually already have.

Happiness is like a butterfly, which when pursued, is always beyond our grasp, but which quietly awaited may alight beside us.

Nathaniel Hawthorne (1800s)

CHAPTER SEVEN

Choosing
"The Right One"

**It is only with the heart that one can
see rightly; what is essential is
invisible to the eye.**

**Antoine de St-Exupery, 1943,
The Little Prince, p. 70**

It HAS ONLY BEEN in the past century or so that romantic love has become the main way to select a mate rather than parental arrangements or selections that are based on rational choice. While choosing "with the heart" quickly became very highly valued in our culture, many believed that attaching this importance to romantic love was actually one of the causes of failures in relationships. On the other hand, finding a partner while at the same time checking off a list of criteria can also be complicated – and certainly gets in the way of the excitement of discovery that is part of the magnetism of romantic love.

The Shopping List

Along with changes in traditional sex role behavior, modern social and economic conditions, and the influence of the mass media, the idealization of romantic love had a dramatic effect on what we are looking for in partners today. At a time for throw-away lovers and searching for our soul-mate, accepting anyone's imperfections is not at all easy. Meeting "The Right One" becomes more and more difficult as we have more and more specific ideas about what we want.

Yet how different are things really? Surveys say, after one's pattering heart has calmed down, women still value intelligence and education and want a man who will work hard in an effort to accomplish something of significance. Men are still more interested in a woman's looks than in her housekeeping or cooking abilities, but they also want her to have order in her life, to work in a systematic way, and to be able to plan ahead. Both believe in the importance of working together to handle difficulties and in the quality of being a nurturing person. When someone acts in an aggressive or humiliating way toward others, it is seen as a warning sign of personality traits that should certainly be avoided. Those who want to have children are particularly concerned about the partner's family values and how they treat their relatives, as well as how they act within the relationship. Those who aren't really interested in having children are usually more concerned about education and economic factors.

There are only two issues that really seem to be new on our modern day selection list. First, while few of us consider chastity prior to the current relationship to be of any importance, both men and women are concerned about having similarity in sex drive and sexual interests. The second new issue is that many of us are worried about discovering — after it is too late — some serious personality problem in a partner. This is a modern sensitivity that possibly comes from our own past experiences within our family or social network, but it might also be a result of the media attention that brings a lot of exposure to many disturbing and frightening personality problems.

Most of us want to select a partner that we can think of as being highly attractive. Usually what this means is someone who is interesting enough to present a challenge but who still leaves us feeling confident that we will have a reasonable chance of succeeding with them. Of course, pursuing this attractive partner requires a sufficient amount of self-esteem. We must be able to see ourselves as attractive enough to impress the other person, making the likelihood of rejection low enough to make it worth the risk of trying.

Individuals tend to choose and prefer partners of approximately their own "social worth," and ... also persist in trying to form relationships with partners who are somewhat more desirable than themselves. ... Thus, it appears that one's romantic choice is a delicate compromise between the realization that one must accept what he or she deserves and the incessant quest for an ideal partner.

Critelli and Waid, 1980, "Physical Attractiveness, Romantic Love, and Equity Restoration in Dating Relationships," p. 625. Journal of Personality Assessment, 44

Marrying Mom or Dad

Many mate selection theories suggest that our childhood relationships provide an unconscious framework for the characteristics that we seek in a partner. Although it is commonly thought that we are most likely to choose a mate resembling our opposite sex parent in some way, there's actually very little evidence that this is true. There is, however, some research evidence (a) that either parent might play a role, (b) that men are more likely to choose someone like their mother than that women will select someone like their father, and (c) that both men and women tend to choose mates that resemble the person who was their main caregiver in childhood.

Freud proposed that marital choice was based on two possibilities. The first was a narcissistic choice, when we choose a partner resembling ourselves, which he said was more likely in women. The second was related to dependency, when we select someone similar to the main person who took care of us as a child, which he said was more likely to influence men. Many studies have been done since then about similarities ("like attracts like") that could be considered supportive of his idea of narcissistic choice even though they were based on conscious factors, like background similarities, not the unconscious issues found in narcissism. But just as many studies say that it's really not similarity but complementarity ("opposites attract") that influences partner selection. This supports Freud's second concept since a complementary partner fulfills our dependent need for something that we feel we lack. Taken all together, the research evidence can be said to support both his proposals: a woman's choice is based on similarity to herself (though this could also mean similarity to her mother or female caregiver) and a man's choice is based on similarity to his childhood caregiver. The conclusion fits, then, that the main caregiver in childhood is the one who influences mate selection in both women and men.

Freudian theory also proposes another factor that probably contributes to our unconscious mate selection process. He said that we often get "stuck" at an early stage of development, either because our progress gets blocked by some upsetting event that happened at the time, or else because some trauma that happens later in life causes us to regress back to that earlier developmental stage. According to this theory, known as the "repetition compulsion," we're likely to unconsciously select a love partner based on our need to repeat this earlier, usually very painful, experience — with the hope, usually unconscious, that somehow this time everything will turn out differently and our past will finally be repaired.

Researchers also looked for evidence about the theory that mate selection could be unconsciously re-creating the childhood relationship with the opposite sex parent rather than based on that parent's appearance or personality traits. Once again, they found this more likely to be based on a primary caregiver relationship rather than on the opposite sex parent relationship. Men were attracted to the qualities of responsiveness and dominance that were similar to their childhood experience, while women sought the qualities of responsiveness and trust that resembled their early caregiver relationship.

Still other theorists said that mate choice might be based on our childhood sense of bonding and then separating (as we establish independence) from our opposite sex parent. According to Object Relations theory, difficulties in adult relationships are based on the failure of our childhood primary "objects" (usually our parents) to create a good bond followed by a secure separation, and then to promote our establishment of a healthy and independent self. One theorist said that if there is <u>intense closeness</u> with the parent without an appropriate separation, this often results in the Don Juan (or the Donna Juanita) syndrome: searching for a perfect mate to replace a "perfect" parent. Each new relationship may start out well, with eager hopefulness and romantic exhilaration, but we end up feeling dissatisfied and disappointed, and then looking for someone else. If our childhood reaction to this intense closeness with our parent was a negative rather than positive one (feeling smothered, for example), the same syndrome might play out as an attempt to get revenge for that overly involved parent. This could include leaving relationships in anger or even with violence. Another theorist has called this response to intense childhood closeness the Cinderella (or Cinderfella) syndrome. We look for a parent figure in a mate, either to replace the positive feeling of connection (like Cinderella's lost father) or to correct for the negative feeling of being smothered (like her controlling stepmother).

If we <u>lacked a close relationship</u> with our opposite sex parent, we therefore also lacked the experience of a healthy separation (a child can't separate appropriately if there hasn't first been sufficient bonding). In this case, our adult inclination could still be one of seeking a parent figure, but either to get revenge for the lack of involvement or to find a substitute who can correct for what was missing.

According to these theorists, it's only when we have had an appropriately high level of closeness followed by a good separation from our opposite sex parent that we are likely to develop into an independent adult who can choose balanced relationships, without the need for either excessive closeness or excessive separateness.

Since mothers traditionally had the main role in nurturing, it was considered less likely that a girl would have this optimal amount of closeness in the relationship with her father, her opposite sex parent. Therefore, in spite of the common notion that women have more expertise in relationships, these theories propose that many women actually <u>lack</u> a positive experience of closeness and healthy separation from the opposite sex. This implies that women are often likely to lack balance in their adult relationships, and may tend to push either toward too much closeness or too much separateness – and maybe even both.

Without this good childhood bonding and individuation, men as well as women are likely to have immature or narcissistic adult relationships that are based on the need to compensate for these unsatisfied aspects of childhood. Adult relationships then tend to be driven by fear of abandonment as well as conflicts about closeness and distance or dependence and independence. Without a healthy differentiation from our parents, our perspective could be so distorted that we might not be able to actually even <u>see</u> the real qualities and limitations of our romantic partner or to be able to accept that partner for the person that they really are.

One more proposed variation on this theme of unconscious mate choices relates to the rest of our family of origin (not just our parents). This theory says that we might be drawn to someone who duplicates the relationship we had with a sibling, or who either duplicates or complements our birth order with our siblings. That is, our attraction will either be to someone with the same birth order (for example, both being the youngest in the family) or else someone who complements our birth order (for example, a man with a younger sister is attracted to a woman with an older brother).

A very attractive woman had a specific "type" that she was always drawn to. Tall, dark, handsome, and strong didn't completely cover it but that was the basic model. In reviewing former boyfriends, they all fit the image, but somehow none of the relationships seemed to work out. We began to examine what this "type" might be all about. Her dad was tall but certainly not handsome. Her mom was dark-haired and good-looking but frail in both body and personality. She didn't really know where her model came from. One day her brother showed up for a visit. He was a combination of the traits of both parents, and, although he was short, he was several

years older so she always looked up to him (physically and emotionally) as a child. As with many sisters and brothers, though, they had become polar opposites about many issues and were not very close as teenagers or young adults. Maybe she had been unconsciously trying to replace her memory of him from childhood, but then, not surprisingly, finding these replacements incompatible. She finally ended up marrying a man who didn't fit her image of a husband at all (a comment that I've heard from <u>many</u> people) and living happily ever after! Once she was able to identify her unconscious thought process and make it conscious by examining it, she was free to choose a mate based on the man himself rather than on the "type" she thought was what she wanted.

On the other hand, many researchers have opposed <u>all</u> of these mom, dad, sister and brother theories, finding that qualities related to parents and siblings (whether they are based on physical appearance, personality traits, or the child-hood relationship) are not really factors in mate selection at all. They believe that, although many of the ideas are theoretically interesting, none of them have proven to be any more likely to occur in mate selection than would be expected by chance.

Opposites Attract

Another theory is one of complementary needs: we tend to choose a mate based on personality traits that are <u>different</u> from our own because it will give us the possibility of getting the most gratification of our needs in life. For example, maybe we choose a high achiever in order to stimulate or compensate for our own overly relaxed style, or we might choose a quiet reserved partner in order to calm down our high need to be social and involved in everything. Being able to figure out what we <u>really</u> need, of course, is a highly complicated process since it's determined by so many external as well as internal, usually unconscious, factors. A passive and dependent man who finds these qualities to be perfectly acceptable in himself might successfully seek out a partner who is strong and nurturing. But if he doesn't accept that these are his qualities and that he could benefit from some complementary traits, then he might instead look for a partner who is similar to himself – and then later resentfully think of her as a "clinging vine."

Carl Jung's theory was a variation on the idea that opposites attract. He thought that we develop models (archetypes) in our unconscious thinking that influence what we search for in a partner. Based on his concept, a man seeks a partner who corresponds to the "anima" archetypal image that he carries within himself which expresses itself as a type of female, while a woman seeks someone who corresponds to her inner "animus" or her male archetypal image. When we find a partner who fits into this internal image, we'll feel as if this person "completes" a missing part of us (maybe generating the expression "my other half").

Birds of a Feather Flock Together

Even though "opposites attract" is what people commonly say, there is actually much more research evidence that supports similarity theories, that "like attracts like" or that we select mates who resemble ourselves. It's less clear how similarities influence our initial attraction to someone, but it has been shown to be significant in the stability of a relationship over a period of time. The most frequently identified items that can predict relationship stability are: similarity in age, intelligence, education (including aspirations for education), physical attractiveness, social class, spirituality or religious beliefs, race, and cultural background. Researchers also said that similarity in where people live was a key factor, finding that couples frequently lived within walking distance of one another when they first met or during early dating. Although the influences of race, religion, and proximity have declined over the past several decades, recent data from dating websites shows that all of these previously identified items are still predictive ingredients in stable lasting relationships.

Similarity in our attitudes and personality traits were also found to be important. People generally lean toward preserving the status quo, maintaining our own traditions, values, and beliefs, so we're likely to select from the same social group as our family of origin. Two other issues that were found to influence whether couples will stay together were similarity in expectations about traditional sex role behavior (what a "wife" does, what a "husband" does) and whether they want to have children, and, if so, how many.

One more similarity that was associated with partnership satisfaction was having a compatible social style (how much we want to be involved with the social environment). At one end of the continuum is the wish to put as much time and energy as possible into just the partnership itself, even acknowledging feeling jealous of outside relationships. At the other end of the continuum is a preference for having a wide variety of outside relationships, each fulfilling different needs but none being dominant or competitive with the primary relationship. The latter social style purposely avoids having just one or two of these outside bonds, probably to consciously minimize any concerns about jealousy. As is the case with many of the issues we encounter in relationships, compatibility of the partners in our stance along the continuum is usually much more important than which particular stance we take.

Still other important similarities found in stable relationships include the amount of social independence that both partners want (that is, how much autonomy we want from being influenced by outsiders), the degree of sensation-seeking both like (that is, how much we want to experience a variety of different things and how willing we are to take risks in order to do so), and whether both have an impulsive or a reflective style of thinking (that is, whether we are likely to reason quickly and spontaneously or slowly and thoughtfully).

Filtering the Eligibles

Probably an optimal match is actually some combination of similar and opposite traits — when it's the right combination. One writer during the 1800s said relationships should be alike with respect to the environment (partners should be similar in purpose and concept about how to live) but complementary with respect to nature (temperament and physical attributes). Two centuries later, contemporary theorists have presented the same basic concept: from within a group of eligible people based on important life similarities, we should choose a mate who complements us in personality characteristics. Research showed that in the short term (eighteen months or less), it was more important to share the same values than it was to have a balance of complementary needs, but for longer relationships the reverse seemed to be true. This finding led to "filter" theories.

Many different theorists proposed a process where initial attraction was based on physical attributes and social status, which was later followed by a filter for similarity in values, and then last by a filter for actually being able to fulfill one another's needs. This final concern probably doesn't enter into consideration any earlier because in the beginning of a relationship we are too busy idealizing it — and one another — to actually be able to see whether it might be able to fulfill any of our long term needs....

So, in the first stage, attraction is based on appearance, social and mental ability, the reputation of both people, and how each one's self-image is able to thrive within the romance (does it nurture feelings of self-esteem or feed fears of failure?). Unless the potential partner passes these initial requirements, it's unlikely that there will be much follow-up. Even if we might be very compatible with respect to our values and needs, we won't ever find this out since we're unlikely to get to that next level.

If we do manage to get past this first filtering process, though, the next stage in the developing relationship involves talking about and comparing our values. A sense of sharing similar values will make us want to share further communication, which will make us feel liked and accepted, which therefore makes us feel more liking and acceptance of our partner.

During the last filtering period, our focus is on the ability of a partner to function in a compatible role. According to this theory, the feeling of "fit" isn't necessarily based on being either similar or complementary, but rather on whether the role of this partner is suitable to our own role and goals. For example, if we are generally self-accepting, we will want our ideal partner to be similar to us, whereas if we are self-conscious about our own weaknesses, we might want a partner who is strong in those qualities that we feel we lack ourselves. As we develop an acceptance of one another, we think of the other as acting in harmony with our own needs and wants. In the absence of any actual evidence to the contrary (and sometimes even when there is evidence to the contrary), we _imagine_ that the partner would be likely to act as we would want them to in a given situation.

This final filtering also takes into account some similarity in both people's feelings of personal adequacy. If we have relatively high self-esteem, we usually won't continue to feel satisfied with someone less adequate. We'll experience a high "cost" of relating to that person and a low "reward" in terms of gains in our own feelings of self-worth. As this imbalance becomes clear, the relationship will most likely end. If our self-esteem is low or we are neurotic in our thinking, we may aim lower in our choices, maybe "settling" for one another, but then all too often ending up later with complications and with both partners having unmet needs. With higher self-esteem and stable non-neurotic thinking, we're more likely to want to have a partner who doesn't make unreasonable demands on us but who can make some, more logical, more easily satisfied demands.

Sexual compatibility is part of this final filter and it's usually more related to being similar in sex drive, sexual interests, and sexual boundaries than in what was experienced prior to the relationship. Research has shown that men with a high sex drive are likely to experience frustration and are less likely to find compatibility in this filtering stage, so they are therefore less likely to progress further in their relationships than are men with a lower sex drive.

Bartering in the Marketplace

According to Exchange Theory, once again, we tend to connect with a mate when there is "distributive justice." That is, when the expected ability of a partner to reward us is about equal to our own ability to be rewarding. If both partners feel that they are rewarding to one another, the relationship is strengthened. When one is insufficiently rewarding, or when this becomes one-sided, the relationship is likely to falter or to end. When there is balance, the difference between a relationship that stays superficial and one that grows into a longer commitment is usually based on how much interdependence develops — how much we are able to change our individual reality in order to incorporate our partner and to develop a couple world view to replace our own individual world view.

Besides considering the rewards and costs of a relationship, other comparisons are taken into account. There is a standard against which we evaluate the relationship (usually based on past relationships) as well as a perception of what other alternatives are still possible. That is, what is acceptable to us in the light of what is available to us. Sometimes we will overlook some imbalance because we don't see any better possibility, perhaps because of our own issues about self-worth, but maybe because there is truly a limited "supply" of possibilities. Or we might have a partner who happens to be very skillful at making us believe there is no one better! In any case, evaluating a particular partner isn't absolute but rather is relative to what else is available. Often exchanges may start out seeming equitable but become unequal over time and then changes need to develop within the relationship in order to restore the balance. There are always a lot of positive and negative exchange items available in a relationship, and, since people and circumstances do frequently change, it might be just a matter of time and effort to find a way to acceptably rebalance the distribution.

According to Behavior Modification or Classical Conditioning Theory (based on positive and negative reinforcement), a couple is more likely to stay together when these exchanges (rewards) are given intermittently rather than continuously (remember the mouse in the maze?). A partner's interest might actually decrease when the rewards are given too often. At the beginning of a relationship, continuous reinforcement is needed ("keeping the fire stoked"), but as things develop, the unpredictability of intermittent reinforcement or rewards does seem to promote endurance. When a relationship blazes quickly but later burns out just as quickly, it is sometimes because of an early surge of continuous rewards that then becomes too much for one or both of the people. And then interest fizzles.

When we persist in a relationship (keeping our own investment and commitment high), we usually find that, over time, our feeling of reward and satisfaction increases, what we are willing to give (our "costs") increases, and our perception of the availability of other high quality partners decreases. We see ourselves as well matched. When we decide instead to leave the relationship, we most likely are experiencing the reverse of this. If we choose not to leave even though we know we're dissatisfied, we may describe the feeling of being trapped, but continue to invest in the relationship anyway, maybe seeing that the alternatives that are available are poor for any number of reasons.

There are also many "escalating" factors, things that will move us toward marriage in spite of relationship imbalances. These include such things as interpersonal addiction (usually based on the fear of being alone), unrealistic fantasies, idealizing the partner or the relationship even in the face of evidence to the contrary, and sometimes a necessity that can't be prevented (an unexpected event like pregnancy or economic difficulties). And then there are some times when we are simply drawn together in spite of what might seem like irreconcilable differences.

One couple was diligently working on several pre-marital concerns so that they could begin to make their wedding plans. They were both excited and nervous, wanting to make a life together but not wanting to make a mistake, something that they had already seen too many of their friends and family doing. Both seemed very committed to the other and determined to build and share a good life. They had grown up in the same town and so had a lot of background similarities as well as compatible goals and beliefs. They hadn't dated for very long but had known one another for a very long time, so they shared a trust and respect for each other, which showed in the way that they cautiously but openly talked over all of their plans and issues. These two were able to examine and resolve concerns related to differences in their personal styles of problem-solving and communication and differences in some of their daily patterns of living, like housekeeping and eating. They could discuss and agree on their desire to have children while still maintaining a good work/life balance. They even cleared up some misunderstandings that they were still carrying from the distant past.

There was one thing that came up as a complete surprise to both of them, however. They came from the East but now lived on the West Coast. His intention was always to stay where they were because of his profession,

friends, and he truly loved the area. She liked it as well but she had always expected to move back East to be near their families, especially if they had children. For many, many weeks they talked this over. Maybe they could stay until she got pregnant and then move. Maybe they could stay and she could visit the family every few months and have them visit in the West as well. Maybe he could find a way to do his work long distance or find something back East that would be just as satisfying. Maybe she could find a job that would make her more interested in staying or she could find friends who were also "transplants" so she'd feel more at home. Maybe they could take a trip East to look for jobs and homes that might encourage him to feel differently. Both of them were shocked that this was an issue. Neither realized the other had a different vision. Every effort that they made to come up with solutions or compromises eventually fell apart. Neither one felt they could give up this essential dream about their future life.

Perhaps another important thing that they learned was about their process of coming to solutions. Throughout their earlier talks, he frequently deferred to her about day-to-day things and she only occasionally deferred to him when something wasn't important to her. Maybe she had just assumed the same would be true with this issue. But this was very important to him. Both were very set in their positions, feeling the other should understand and should give in. Each felt the other should want what was best for them. In spite of seeing the consequence, there seemed to be no way out. Neither was willing to change. Irreconcilable differences. Fortunately, this was before the wedding had been planned so they still had time to separate and think it over. Sometimes there is no way to resolve a difference and you have to accept defeat. And sometimes that may be for the best.

No, I don't know what the eventual outcome was, whether they separated for good or got together again. We have to leave this ending up to our imaginations. But I think if one partner gets used to always getting their way it may eventually leave the relationship unbalanced. Both need to have some areas of control or deference. But it is up to <u>both</u> partners to make sure this will be the case.

CHAPTER EIGHT

When You See A Stranger...

**Boy meets girl and if the chemistry is right
courtship follows ... the usual courting
behavior involving a myriad of ploys and
counterploys whereby each lover beguiles,
entices, cajoles, and mesmerizes the other
with posturing and flattery....**

**Bakker and Bakker-Rabdau, 1973,
<u>No Trespassing</u>, p. 82**

WE USUALLY MAKE UP our minds quickly about potential partners and screen them out if they don't generate that vague concept we know as "chemistry" or if they don't fit our mold for Mr. or Ms. Right. Maybe they have some visible flaw in their appearance or in their behavior; maybe they're somewhat awkward in initially forming relationships or in making casual conversation; maybe they're just too eager — or maybe even just too nice. In spite of the possibilities that they may hold underneath these imperfections, they are passed over, because, though they might make secure and wonderful companions, they just have no "sizzle." Some people think this highly sought-after phenomenon is actually the nervousness and uncertainty that goes along with not knowing how the other person is feeling about us. Others theorize that this seemingly divinely inspired "click" with that "stranger across a crowded room" is actually a "transference" reaction (that the person unconsciously reminds us of someone from our past) – in which case we should probably run as fast as we can in the other direction! However, in spite of all of the warnings and theories, chemistry continues to be valued highly in initial attraction.

Beyond this unexplainable physiological feeling, those stimulating features about another person (some combination of how they look, how they act, what they say, and what they know or believe) generate a certain picture about that person which can lead to feelings of attraction. Deciding whether to pursue this seemingly gravitational force then comes from some combination of our own sense of self-esteem at that moment, our anticipation of whether we are likely to get a positive response, and whether or not the probability of future interaction seems high enough to make it worth the effort.

How They Look

A woman was attending a language class that met weekly and had noticed a very attractive man glancing at her on several occasions. She quietly smiled and looked away, thinking that, if he were interested, he would make some move to interact with her. But he never did. Though she was far from plain looking, she wasn't confident enough to approach him because she was so intimidated by his good looks. One day he showed up in class with a bad rash covering his face and neck and she overheard him talking about catching poison ivy when he went camping. Not looking quite so handsome now, he no longer felt so intimidating. And, she was a nurse! The next time they exchanged a glance, she smiled slightly and passed him a note with a treatment for the rash. His thank you began their first conversation.

Most research on attraction shows that we attribute positive personal qualities to people who are attractive physically. This is true whether we're evaluating others of the same sex or the opposite sex. Appearance has been shown to be a significant factor in success, whether in business, getting promotions, forming friendships, choosing a mate, or long-term marital happiness. We see attractive people as more responsible, as higher in self-esteem, and as more socially confident than less attractive people. Their opinions and evaluations are given more attention and tend to have more impact on others. They are also more likely to get preferential treatment, help, and responsiveness from others. There seems to be only one positive trait that we do not disproportionately attribute to attractive people and that is level of honesty!

We also tend to attribute positive qualities and higher status to someone who is associated with a physically attractive person. We are judged by the company we keep! A man, especially a physically unattractive one, is seen more favorably when he is with an attractive woman. Either we assume he has other positive qualities to attract the partner (Exchange Theory) or we attribute the woman's favorable characteristics to him as well (the "halo effect"). This tends to be different for women, however. We often think of a woman as more likable when she is with an unattractive rather than an attractive man. We may think of her priorities as more admirable (although we often measure men in wealth, not looks), or maybe she just seems less threatening.

Research shows that we interact differently with someone we find attractive in a way that then perpetuates our stereotype. For example, when we present ourselves to someone attractive in an admiring way, we're likely to see their response as consistent with our expectation. We believe the person will react in a likable, confident way – and then they do.

Studies also show that when we find one another physically attractive right away, we're much more likely to make the effort to get to know one another better. Also, if we are similar to one another in attractiveness, we're more likely to develop the relationship and have it continue to progress. Although the appearance factor usually decreases in importance after we get to know one another, if it was initially a high priority, it is highly likely that dissatisfaction will develop if the partner's appearance changes very much. If a woman is physically unattractive, she's seen as less desirable than an unattractive man, so this can become especially problematic with aging. Older women often have difficulty maintaining a positive self-image because the standard of beauty for women is based on having an appealing, and youthful, appearance.

One important factor that is associated with attractiveness in men is height, and men who are tall are more likely to attract partners who are better looking than they are. However, tall men who see themselves as overly thin, as well as men and women who see themselves as overweight, often have difficulty in forming romantic relationships. Maybe they don't see themselves as attractive enough to deserve someone else's attention and so they sabotage themselves. Once they do get involved, though, their own perception of their attractiveness is often strengthened by the relationship itself.

Researchers also found that we tend to see our partners as more attractive than ourselves. Maybe this is because of the notion that "love is blind" and so the beloved is always beautiful — or maybe because we all want to believe we've made a good "bargain" in the "marketplace of love." If we really do believe our partner is more attractive than we are, we also often have the sense that we love them more than they love us, and have the insecure feeling that we are the more submissive one in the relationship. If we think that we are the one who is more attractive, we're less likely to worry that our partner will get involved with someone else, but we're more likely (especially men) to be vulnerable to, or maybe even to seek, the attention of others.

Perhaps one of the more complicating difficulties related to this issue is that our overwhelming exposure to the mass media has so impacted our standards for physical attractiveness that many of us have truly unrealistic expectations. As a consequence, we're often dissatisfied with those people who are actually available to us, as well as with ourselves.

How They Act

Flirting involves largely the expression of attraction ... designed to elicit some commitment from the other in advance of making a serious commitment oneself.

**Peter Blau, 1974,
Exchange and Power in Social Life, p. 227**

Men are often hesitant to approach women without some indication of interest from them first, so some initial non-verbal interaction is usually important in attraction. This "flirting" can be from very subtle to quite obvious, but the essence of it involves an appearance of ambivalence: tentative and hesitant signals of approach and withdrawal. As discussed previously, some approach-avoidance signals can be discouraging and even rude, but most flirting behavior seems to maintain the sense of interest – a thread of connection – even while it may look like withdrawal. It includes smiling briefly at the other person; gazing at them and then looking away; putting our hand on our face while glancing at them; or just maintaining some demure facial expression, modest and not too aggressive for men, shy and cautiously receptive for women.

If we want to encourage flirting attention, we can re-orient our body a little in the direction of the initiator; or gaze back briefly and then look quietly downward (but not to the side since this signals that we're diverting our attention elsewhere); or just sit still as a cue that the initiator won't be rejected if advances are made. If, instead, we want to discourage the flirting attention, we should withhold eye contact; re-orient our position away from the person; look off to the side; stare back briefly, but blankly, and without smiling; or tilt our head slightly backwards. Unfortunately, we sometimes react like this out of insecurity or discomfort, not meaning to be discouraging at all, not realizing that we may be sabotaging further interaction whether we want it or not.

Many times we aren't even aware of the signals that we're sending and sometimes we get a response that is not what we were looking for at all. This frequently happens if we are unconsciously or unintentionally acting seductive, and then we're left wondering why we're getting attention that is more aggressive than what we want ("But I'm not that kind of a girl!"). Of course, seductiveness can also be in the eyes of the beholder, when nothing is actually being signaled at all.

Being able to accurately send and read flirting cues certainly doesn't guarantee confidence in initial interactions or success in dating, but it can help with understanding the "game" a little better. We often say that we don't want to have to play games to get a partner, we just want to be "authentic." Or, if it's "meant to be" then tactics shouldn't be necessary. That may be true. But if we wanted to know how to successfully present ourselves for a job interview, we would probably want to learn a good approach and be prepared with some things that we want to say. While authenticity is probably the most important presentation to strive for in relationships, perhaps some parts of authenticity can also be learned. This can include such things as manners, tact, sensitivity, charisma, and an understanding of human nature.

Research has shown several factors to be important in a fairly universal system of non-verbal signals that we use in negotiating relationships: physical space, posture and gesture, and facial expressions and eye contact.

Physical space. Sometimes attraction is related to simply having some exposure to a person over a period of time. Being nearby physically increases the likelihood that we will interact with someone, which then increases our familiarity, which usually leads to liking. Negotiating our physical space within this exposure, though, can be a vital factor. Maintaining a body distance of three to five feet is what is generally considered suitable for casual interaction (although this distance varies from culture to culture). For more intimate interaction, the distance is about eighteen inches. The timing that's involved in decreasing this distance is critical to the success of the relationship. Any attempt to get closer needs to coincide with signs of willingness from the other person. Traditionally, a woman would maintain a casual interaction distance from a man, and the man would have to be the one to daringly (or annoyingly) move closer. More recently, women have been described as more likely to "invade" the man's personal space. While some men say they enjoy this behavior, others say they find it threatening. With actual touching, however, women are usually the ones expected to initiate this. Women tend to touch other women more than men touch other men. Most women say they like some physical touch but men are less consistent about it. For both men and women, responding to touching usually depends on where we're being touched, what the surrounding circumstances and the environment look like, and how we already see the relationship.

Posture and gesture. How we orient our body can signal either that we want to increase intimacy (facing toward the person although not directly head-on) or maintain our distance (facing away from the person but without necessarily turning our back). A receptive, non-threatening pose conveys the message of wanting to encourage intimacy. This includes raising our eyes to meet the other person's eyes, tipping our head slightly toward the other person, holding our own arms or neck with our hands, casually folding our arms across our abdomen, or slightly flexing our shoulders.

Facial expressions and eye contact. Facial expressions that show fear, surprise, uncertainty, or anger are likely to make other people feel uncomfortable. If we minimize this and instead send signals of warmth and attentiveness, our attractiveness increases.

In casual one-to-one interaction, women are more likely to attempt to make eye contact, laugh or smile, while men are more likely to avoid these. This may be because women are more comfortable in face-to-face pairs while men are more at ease in groups or side-by-side interactions. As intimacy grows, eye contact and smiling increase. Couples who are "in love" can frequently be found wrapped up in mutual gazing....

What They Say

A midlife widowed man was afraid of trying to meet new people because he was worried about not knowing what to say. This improved with practice and with the help of a fun story about a very famous couple. When these two were in graduate school together, he was already aware of her and she had a reputation for being quite brilliant. One day the school was having a special luncheon for all of the classes, and while the woman was fixing herself a plate of food, she noticed this very handsome man kept looking at her. She decided to just walk over to him and introduce herself. He just stood there and stared at her. So she asked him what his name was. But he continued to stand there, smiling blankly and staring. He finally did speak, but much later he did admit that he was so awed he couldn't remember his own name!

Fear of meeting people can be similar to having to give a presentation to an audience. It helps when you rehearse the first few minutes of what you are going to say until it feels very comfortable and natural. Then, once you are past that starting point, it's much easier to continue with more spontaneity. This widowed man rehearsed several items of small talk and also learned to focus his attention on the other person, getting them to talk, realizing that they might also be feeling unsure about what to say.

Our verbal communication includes the actual content of what's being said, how it is being said, and also the process of personal bonding that's taking place at the same time as the conversation. Sometimes the content isn't even relevant to the formation of the bond. It isn't always <u>what</u> is being said but just the sharing of the interaction.

But there is one particular type of content in verbal communication that has been extensively researched and found to be very influential in the development of personal relationships. This is called "self-disclosure," revealing personal things about ourselves. In general, attraction leads to self-disclosure, which breaks down barriers and we then allow ourselves to be further vulnerable. That vulnerability often leads to romantic love. The success of this sequence depends both on our timing and whether the disclosures are positive or negative in nature. For example, if we talk about good fortune too early in a relationship, it can be seen as unattractive if it sounds like boasting. It depends on how we express it as well as whether it was something that we earned or if it was just the result of good luck. If we've had some bad fortune, and we feel personally responsible for it having a negative outcome, we're seen as more attractive if we disclose it relatively early in the relationship because we'll seem to be letting ourselves be open rather than trying to conceal something. On the other hand, if we aren't seen as responsible for the misfortune anyway, we'll usually be better liked if we disclose it later on when it won't be seen as a play for sympathy. In any case, <u>too much</u> disclosure too soon can scare away a potential partner, but <u>too little</u> can lead to a sense of detachment, which can produce discomfort or suspicion or complicated misunderstandings rather than developing trust.

One woman was being very understanding about how her new boyfriend hadn't gotten a job that he was pursuing. She knew that he was distraught and she was trying to be supportive so she told him that he had certainly done the best that he could. This was a big relief to him and so he was glad that he had told her about it. She didn't reveal her anxiety as he continued to bring up different issues, though, and her feelings were being bottled up under her self-imposed guise of trying to be reasonable. At a later point, she became frustrated about some very small thing that was completely unrelated. Suddenly her feelings all came bubbling out. She felt he had been overlooked for

**the job because he hadn't been willing to compromise —
something she was worried about in their relationship as
well. She hadn't told him that she knew someone at the
company where he had applied; that she had heard that
he was unwilling to accept what they <u>did</u> offer him. She
had been carrying this thought around in her head while
they discussed other things, from what they liked to eat
for dinner to their hopes and dreams for their lives. She
didn't tell him that her own biggest fear, irrational as she
knew it was, was about being unemployed and ending up
living (and even dying) in the street, something that had
actually happened to a friend of hers. Being reasonable
and understanding is an important part of a relationship,
but so is being open about one's feelings and fears.**

Reciprocity is a crucial issue in this process of self-disclosure. Research found, for example, that a woman who matches a partner's level of intimacy in disclosing is more likable than one who responds with too much intimacy (and then might be seen as being overly emotional) or one who fails to reciprocate (and then might be seen as indifferent or cold). Since most men and women still follow traditional sex role expectations when it comes to self-disclosure, the woman may have to gently pave the way. Even the more "liberated" men still don't like to disclose weaknesses, and this reluctance is reinforced, because when they do, women often react with disappointment, withdrawing their admiration. They're afraid that they won't be able to count on the man to lean on if they need him. Similarly, women are often reluctant to disclose their strengths, and this is reinforced, because when they do, men often react negatively, feeling intimidated or challenged and seeming to withdraw in their role as the protector. Typically, men are seen as likable and better adjusted if they don't disclose much personal information. The opposite is true for women. Many men <u>say</u> that they want women to be open and to talk with them in the same unedited way that they talk with other women — but they may get tired of listening. Many women <u>say</u> that they want men to be open and self-disclosing — but they may be ambivalent about the result.

What happens when the disclosure is about previous relationships? Even though this might be intended to just describe a chapter of our past history, it generally carries much deeper implications. It might be a hint about how a relationship is supposed to be or how it's not supposed to be, or a justification of our own limitations, or an attempt to artificially create emotional closeness or distance, or it can even be a warning about the possible destiny of the new relationship. Too much talking about or thinking about past partners sometimes preserves the past while interfering with the growth of the present relationship. To the listener, the previous partner becomes someone to be measured against, arousing all kinds of feelings of competition, fears of having the same outcome, resentments, unhealthy curiosity, undue sympathy, or even empathy or admiration for them. Not talking at all about past partners can have the advantage of leaving a "blank slate" so as not to arouse all of those feelings. However, it also runs the risk of seeming too withholding unless we are able to balance it adequately with openness in other areas of disclosure.

The scope of how we reveal ourselves is measured by the range of topics that we discuss, how personal or private the topics are, the extensiveness of our descriptions, and how positively or negatively our thoughts are presented and judged. As intimacy increases, all of these areas tend to increase. If intimacy later decreases, we're likely to restrict the topics we're willing to discuss, but we might actually increase how deeply or how personally we get into those areas that we do want to discuss. We're also likely to be less positive in evaluating the things that the partner is saying, often with more and more negative judgments occurring as a result of the loss of intimacy.

What They Know or Believe

When we share similar attitudes and values with someone else, this supports our own sense of self-worth and makes us feel hopeful about our future compatibility with that person. Our similarity is positively reinforcing and results in wanting to continue to invest further in the new partnership.

Since education is one of the main predictors of our attitude about relationships, being similar in education is usually an important part of compatibility. Also, similarity in competence is a major factor, including both our aspirations and our capabilities. Men are often seen as feeling threatened by competence in a woman, but this fear is actually more likely to be related to her aspirations rather than her competence, especially when these aspirations involve roles or occupations that have traditionally been considered masculine. On the other hand, a man usually admires a woman's <u>capability</u>, and he won't find her less attractive because she is success oriented, especially if her interests might enhance and not compete with his own.

Research also shows that men who believe female competence is threatening are actually likely to improve their own performance on a task when they are in a competitive situation with a competent female partner. Afterwards, though, they may try to avoid doing tasks together in the future, saying they prefer to work individually. If a man who doesn't feel threatened by competence in women is put into this same competition with a female partner, he'll either improve his performance or stay the same, but afterwards he won't show any wish to avoid working together on future tasks. Women with traditional sex role beliefs tend to perform less well when they compete against a male partner than when they work cooperatively with him. The reverse is true for a non-traditional woman. The competition improves her performance.

When we see a very competent man or woman making a mistake, it often makes us think of them as <u>more</u> attractive. If we see an average person spilling their coffee during a meeting, this might decrease their attractiveness to us. But when we see someone who is highly competent doing exactly the same thing, spilling coffee, their attractiveness is increased. This is also true when a highly competent person experiences a tragedy or a difficult circumstance, especially if they aren't responsible for it themselves. We seem to see that person as more human, more approachable, and their attractiveness increases, even though that is usually not the case for someone who is considered less competent. We're more likely instead to see them as the poor, maybe even inept, victim.

Two other values that have been shown to influence attractiveness in a potential partner are their religious involvement (or spiritual beliefs) and prior sexual experience. Having similarity in religious belief has been shown to influence the early phase of dating as well as to continue to be important in long-term success in relationships. This can be sharing some form of spirituality or metaphysical thinking or some involvement in special traditions, without necessarily being connected to a particular religious affiliation. With respect to sexuality, studies have shown that people with less experience prefer either inexperienced or moderately experienced partners. For those who have had experience themselves, women tend to prefer a partner who is also more experienced, but for men the amount of experience of a partner is not particularly relevant.

Chapter Nine

The Dance
Of Relationship

"I cannot play with you," the fox said. "I am not tamed."

"Ah! Please excuse me," said the little prince. ...

"What does that mean – 'tame'?" ...

"It is an act too often neglected," said the fox. "It means to establish ties."

"'To establish ties'?"

"Just that," said the fox. "To me, you are still nothing more than a little boy who is just like a hundred thousand other little boys. And I have no need of you. And you, on your part, have no need of me. To you, I am nothing more than a fox like a hundred thousand other foxes. But if you tame me, then we shall need each other. To me, you will be unique in all the world. To you, I shall be unique in all the world . . ."

"I am beginning to understand," said the little prince. "There is a flower . . . I think that she has tamed me . . ."

... "One only understands the things that one tames," said the fox. "Men have no more time to understand anything. They buy things all ready made at the shops. But there is no shop anywhere where one can buy friendship, and so men have no friends any more. If you want a friend, tame me . . ."

"What must I do, to tame you?" asked the little prince.

"You must be very patient," replied the fox. "First you will sit down at a little distance from me – like that – in the grass. I shall look at you out of the corner of my eye, and you will say nothing. Words are the source of misunderstandings. But you will sit a little closer to me, every day . . ."

The next day the little prince came back.

"It would have been better to come back at the same hour," said the fox. "If, for example, you came at four o'clock in the afternoon, then at three o'clock I shall begin to be happy. I shall feel happier and happier as the hour advances. At four o'clock, I shall already be worrying and jumping about. I shall show you how happy I am! But if you come at just any time, I shall never know at what hour my heart is to be ready to greet you . . . One must observe the proper rites . . ." . . .

[Later the little prince sees some roses in a garden.]

"You are beautiful, but you are empty." . . . "One could not die for you. To be sure, an ordinary passerby would think that my rose looked just like you – the rose that belongs to me. But in herself alone she is more important than all the hundreds of you other roses: because it is she that I have watered; because it is she that I have put under the glass globe; because it is she that I have sheltered behind the screen; because it is for her that I have killed the caterpillars (except two or three that we saved to become butterflies); because it is she that I have listened to, when she grumbled, or boasted, or even sometimes when she said nothing. Because she is my rose." . . .

"It is the time you have wasted for your rose that makes your rose so important." . . . "You become responsible, forever, for what you have tamed." . . .

[Later in his journey, after leaving the fox, he thought back on his new friend and the little prince said] One runs the risk of weeping a little, if one lets himself be tamed . . .

Antoine de St-Exupery, 1943,
The Little Prince, excerpts from pp. 65-71, 81

IT IS SAID THAT psychological health requires an ability to form the deep and lasting relationships that can provide our life with a framework of understanding and safety so that we're able to grow and explore. Research shows the benefit of having a "significant other" during the stressful times of life and some theorists even go so far as to say that we aren't able to really experience our own existence unless it's within the context of our relationships with others.

So what is it that affects the development of relationships and why does it seem to be different for some of us than it is for others? Why do some of us "establish ties" with a life partner while some of us do not?

There are many factors and variables that arise from both our internal influences (individual personality characteristics) and our external influences (family, friends, and society). The following are some that are prominent in the social-psychology research. Most of us fall somewhere along the middle of the continuum on the issues, or we might even have parts of ourselves at each end of the continuum, but these are the influences and traits that generally differentiate us from one another.

Internal Influences

PURSUING AND DISTANCING

One personality trait that strongly influences the development of relationships is the phenomenon related to pursuing and distancing. At one end of this continuum are those of us who are always seeking excitement or stimulation through social interaction. We are called "pursuers." Our actions include dramatic emotional displays, efforts at seduction, and dependency oriented involvements (or perhaps "entanglements" is a better description). We seek togetherness, we don't like being alone, and we are often embroiled in some relationship problem. We blur the boundaries in relationships and we seem to need to fill some inner sense of emptiness. Those of us who are "distancers" are at the other end of this continuum. We are trying to avoid social stimulation as much as possible and suppress our interpersonal feelings. When we do relate to others, we're focused on issues about rejection and withdrawal, passivity and negativism. We obsess about details. We are seeking individuality, we want to have our privacy, and we want to avoid any emotional involvement in order to protect ourselves.

These two personality types (also known as "hysterical" and "obsessive") often are attracted to one another because of these complementary styles. We each initially idealize the other because we see what we are lacking in ourselves. So the warm, vital, loving, fun, spontaneous, empathic hysteric is drawn to the controlled, intellectualized, profound, organized, strong, successful obsessive. But…, later on in the relationship (as is often true with qualities that we're initially attracted to), these opposing styles can lead to serious frustration and conflict. Then comes the question: why can't he or she be more like me?

One personality theorist proposed a similar phenomenon but using three styles instead of two: moving toward, moving against, and moving away from. Those of us who "move toward" other people give the appearance of being helpless, needing to win the affection of others so that we can lean on them. We act compliant, doing what others want us to do, in order to gain a sense of support and belonging. Those of us who tend to "move against" others live our lives based on the assumption that we are surrounded by hostility and therefore must be prepared and determined to fight at any time. We are rebellious and mistrusting of everyone, expecting that no one can ever understand us or assist us. The third style, those of us who "move away from" others, aren't interested in either belonging or in fighting. We just simply want to be separate. Often we even stay estranged from ourselves and numb to any emotional experience. We can get along well superficially, but we get anxious when we feel that others are intruding on us. We want to be independent and self-sufficient, and will often restrict our own needs in order to achieve this. We enjoy being alone, we require a lot of privacy, and we often seem as if we feel that we are somehow superior or unique.

SELF-MONITORING

A second trait that influences relationship development is how "self-monitoring" we tend to be. Those of us who are highly self-monitoring are those whose behavior is based on cues that we get (or think we get) from others. We're likely to be the ones who initiate interactions, often speaking first in a conversation and then directing the action of whatever happens, but we do it while tailoring our behavior to suit our partner. We're likely to date different people for short periods of time, remaining uncommitted, with a sense that we'll end the relationship at any given time if it no longer suits us. We're very conscious of being socially appropriate and concerned about controlling the image that we (and our partner) are projecting to others. This makes us very sensitive to negative changes in our partner. For example, a change in a partner's physical appearance could easily jeopardize the relationship. The personality that is known as "Type A" is included in this group – ambitious, high-strung, and often very successful at work, but much less successful at being able to maintain enduring personal relationships.

Those of us with high self-monitoring personalities usually choose friends that fit in with a particular activity that interests us, which often ends up being an unstable way to choose since our interests frequently change. We view marriage as a partnership built around a mutual sharing of activities – in other words, a relationship based on what we are doing together.

Low self-monitoring types are more concerned with internal issues, like attitudes, values, and personality traits, so we're more likely to choose friends just because we like and feel liked by them. For us, the longer a relationship continues, the more acceptance and intimacy develop – which is exactly what we want. We see marriage as a partnership centered around being together, with the emphasis on being. If we end a relationship, it's usually because our partner has changed in some significant way that now makes his or her personality less desirable to be around.

SELF-ESTEEM

A third personality factor, and possibly the most important in its impact on how we develop relationships, is self-esteem. Theorists talk about "self-actualization" (like the military slogan "Be all that you can be," but here referring to the psychological self), saying that those of us who are self-accepting and are not defensive are more capable of loving others and experiencing satisfying and fulfilling relationships. This personality type tends to be cautious about being receptive to romantic love, but is more likely to be successful at it.

Those with low self-esteem have a strong need for affection and confirmation of our own worthiness, which can get in the way of relating in the long term. We tend to be easily receptive to romantic love, falling in love frequently and experiencing euphoria, maybe out of our own strong need for affirmation. We express great love and trust for a partner and usually evaluate them more favorably than we evaluate ourselves. We select a mate that we think will enhance our own ideal self, but of whom we often actually feel unworthy, so then we end up fearing that the love is unbalanced. On the other hand, we also often experience the opposite problem of this sense of imbalance. Sometimes our sense of unworthiness leads us to "settle" for someone and we later resent it, feeling like we could have done better.

When our self-esteem is vulnerable, the protective mechanism of defensiveness comes out, which then inhibits the kind of exploration that is one of the phases of a love relationship. The prospect of having to reveal ourselves as intimacy develops is much too threatening since we fear that we'll be rejected once we're "found out." Because of this, defensive people have fewer, and more guarded, experiences of romantic love.

Vulnerable self-esteem also sometimes presents itself as social anxiety. This can happen when we see the possibility of rejection in a highly exaggerated way, usually due to a catastrophic style of thinking. People who are socially confident also get rejected, of course, but are able to put it into perspective, not focusing on self-blaming thoughts.

Sometimes we try to maintain self-esteem by using a form of "self-handicapping." That is, we emphasize the unfortunate events and experiences we've had in our life as a way of giving ourselves an excuse in advance for any potential failure. For example, not all of us suffer in the same way from the shock of any particular trauma, so we might try, usually unconsciously, to make out of it whatever will suit our purposes. We describe a past trauma as a way of avoiding responsibility for our current inability to succeed.

MASCULINITY/FEMININITY

Still another personality measure that can significantly affect a relationship is the continuum of what is considered to be typically masculine and what is considered to be typically feminine. So do macho men or highly feminine women make better partners? Actually, studies show that those of us who are androgynous (have a mix of masculine and feminine traits) are usually more loving than those of us who are sex-role stereotyped. We seem to be more aware of our feelings, more willing to express our feelings, and more tolerant of the faults of our partner than those of us who are either highly masculine or highly feminine. We're less likely to compromise the differing aspects of our personality, the anima-animus, the yin-yang, our strength and our tenderness. We express both of these sides. When this is in balance, it seems to minimize a woman's fear of rejection for being too strong and a man's fear of vulnerability for being too soft.

MATURITY

The last, but certainly not the least, issue that deserves mention in discussing personality traits that influence relationship success is our ability — and willingness — to actually achieve adulthood. This often gets in the way in the dance of relationship. While it can be helpful for us to hold onto some of the childlike behaviors that make life playful and fun, perpetuating some of our childish or adolescent behaviors and traits is more likely to do serious damage in our long-term commitments: moodiness, touchiness, egocentric self-indulgence, being excessively idealistic or romanticizing, or getting into power and authority struggles.

External Influences

Grown-ups love figures. When you tell them that you have made a new friend, they never ask you any questions about

essential matters. They never say to you,
"What does his voice sound like? What
games does he love best? Does he collect
butterflies?" Instead, they demand: "How
old is he? How many brothers has he?
How much does he weigh? How much
money does his father make?" Only from
these figures do they think they have
learned anything about him.

Antoine de St-Exupery, 1943,
The Little Prince, p.17-18

SUPPORT AND INTERFERENCE

Support (or the lack of it) from our own family and friends can play an important role in the success or failure of a romantic involvement. The likelihood of a relationship progressing is at least partially determined by having this support, along with both partners being liked by and liking the family and friends of the other, and having some amount of contact and communication with them. As our romantic involvement develops, we have a tendency to decrease our involvement with our friends, but to maintain or even increase our family relationships.

In general, our friends and relatives (especially our roommates and mothers) will promote activities that enhance the development of a relationship – but only until we are close to making a commitment! Then, these very same people begin trying to influence us in the other direction, trying to get us away from one another. This can discourage a relationship, but it can also trigger the Romeo and Juliet effect (or from Ovid's Pyramus and Thisbe, "the more a flame is covered up, the hotter it burns"). While interference is undermining our trust and stability in the relationship, the paradox is that it also pushes us closer together to depend on one another for emotional support, out of the need to unite against this unanticipated common enemy.

One couple was delaying getting married until they both lost a certain amount of weight that they agreed would represent the healthy lifestyle that they wanted to live together. At first this goal made the weight-loss easier for the man because he felt committed to both the woman and to being healthy. However, every time he was making significant progress, his family would throw a party or an event that made it really hard for him to resist indulging. Although he wanted to please his fiancé, it was his family that he was even more accustomed to pleasing. And they seemed determined to sabotage his efforts. Meanwhile, his fiancé had her own fears of commitment and seemed to be unconsciously sabotaging the goal as well, keeping alive in her mind the rationalization that they might break up and she would then run off with some fantasy version of her truly perfect mate. Eventually the man recognized that making a commitment to such a personal goal had to be out of a desire to please himself, not anyone else, so his first goal needed to be standing up to his family. His fiancé also admitted to her own fears and then, together, they were able to encourage each other's commitment to their plan, with each helping the other focus on what was working rather than blaming the partner for what wasn't. She was also able to let him know that she respected his strong stance with his family, and felt it was an important step in paving their path to a healthy future together.

EARLY FAMILY EXPERIENCE

Parents see the pressure and expectations that they put on their children to get married as their way of being encouraging or protective. They insist it isn't just because they want to have grandchildren or because they want to be relieved of their caretaker responsibilities! Sometimes, however, their underlying motivation can actually be much more obscure and unconscious: they are afraid that their children's failure to marry is actually a measure of failure in their own life.

To what extent does our experience in our family of origin influence our future relationships? Research shows that our perceptions about marriage, as well as many of our relationship behaviors that are pathological, are, in fact, transmitted from the family. Those of us who score high on viewing our family of origin as healthy also score high on our perceptions about marriage. But the opposite is also true, especially if we had any exposure to parental violence, or to highly stressful disharmony even without violence. The effects of being deprived of one or both of our parents because of divorce or the effects of being exposed to parental violence are always difficult to observe because of the complexity of life, but many studies have concluded that there are problems that do persist into adulthood, increasing our likelihood of having depression, aggression, and anxiety. Other researchers, however, have concluded that these problems should be attributed to other life circumstances or to other background factors, arguing that most negative effects of parental divorce decreased when the divorce rate increased. That is, as more people became divorced, the effect on each child became less noticeable.

One study found that when a woman's parents had been unhappily married but stayed together anyway, the woman was actually less likely to feel that she herself was ever going to get married than were women with happily married parents or parents who were unhappy but separated or divorced. Both men and women from divorced families were found to have a high frequency of dating (but often with poor relationship quality) when they were from a home with a lot of obvious conflict, or when the parent they lived with stayed single for a long time, or when their own relationship with either or both of their parents deteriorated after the divorce. Maybe this high frequency of dating might be from anxiously trying to correct the situation through their own adult relationships — but without the right tools to do so. While some of these effects decreased significantly after divorce rates increased, maybe this was because the children were exposed to less anger and violence.

As a very young child, a woman recalls, her parents were arguing viciously almost every night after they thought she was asleep. Sometimes she heard someone falling or something breaking but mostly it was shouting and As a very young child, a woman recalls, her parents were arguing viciously almost every night after they thought she was asleep. Sometimes she heard someone falling or something breaking but mostly it was shouting and anger, muffled but still piercing through the walls. She had two dolls, a boy doll and a girl doll, and every night she tried having them talk to each other or having them hug each other, always placing them in a different position next to each other for the night, thinking through her tears that if only she could get them into the right position, maybe her parents would stop fighting. As an adult, she found herself in a relationship with a man who often used his temper to get what he wanted from business associates, sales people, hotel clerks, waiters, and so on. One time they were in a car with friends and he began arguing with the driver. When he couldn't get his way, he suddenly jumped out of the car and walked home.... And then one night he turned his temper on her. She sat frozen in her chair, afraid to change position, afraid to say anything, tears streaming down her face. Finally, exasperated, he left. After quite a while, she managed to get up, realizing that it was over. She made herself a cup of tea, a little surprised at how calm she was, and smiled as the thought crossed her mind of having her dolls join her at the table, each in its own chair, chatting amiably. She realized that this was now her kitchen — it didn't have to include that kind of conflict. Not long after that, she met a new man, gentle in nature, assertive in a mild-mannered way, a man who could openly express his own feelings and get her to express herself as well ... compassionately. And he even loved sitting at her kitchen table and drinking tea!

Losing a parent in early childhood due to serious illness, disability, or death (or even the feeling of loss because of some traumatic event like the parent losing their job or suddenly needing to move) also influences future adult relationships, depending on the age of the child, the way the circumstance was handled by the family, and the responsibilities that were then pressed onto the child.

One other type of loss occurs when we discover that a parent is less all-powerful than our idealized version of them as our protector. This normally happens when we're able to take on more and more functions ourselves and have less need to rely on them. But sometimes this disillusionment takes place too early or too quickly, before we are really ready to adapt to it. This sometimes results in our taking on a false sense of our own grandiosity (because now we have to become the all-powerful and all-knowing) or else in our continual search for that lost idealized parent figure, possibly accounting for the search for the "ideal" mate.

After dating several women, a divorced man began to see that, although they all looked different, they all seemed to have some personality traits that were very similar to his ex-wife, something that he had been trying to avoid. He began thinking that it must be his own fault. He could probably start out with _any_ woman and turn her into one with those unwanted qualities: dependent on him to take care of her, wanting him to make all the decisions, and all the while being self-absorbed, overly critical, and unable to see his needs at all. From the time he was a child, he had been very good at fixing things and at keeping things in order, often out of necessity because his parents were not doing it. They praised him for these talents, but also took advantage of him — and then blamed him if anything went wrong. He was often left "in charge" of his younger brother and sister and his parents would go out drinking and partying. He hadn't actually been abandoned, but he did have to become the all-knowing protector in order to provide some sense of security for his siblings and for himself. Now, in his adult relationships with women (and, he thought, at work, too) he saw that he

kept taking that on again and again. He "trained" women to expect him to do everything and think that he wanted nothing in return. Then he felt taken advantage of. And lonely. Now it was time to train himself. He needed to be able to express his needs, let others take the lead, and <u>allow</u> himself to be the one who was being taken care of some of the time.

One other potential cause of difficulty in forming adult attachments is when deep unresolved grief interferes with our ability to be open to new relationships, especially if the event of grieving occurred in our childhood. Many things can keep us from resolving this grief. Maybe we don't have anyone to share it with or a support network to comfort us. Or we think we have to assume the role of the "strong one" or to be the one to keep things under control. Or we have ambivalent feelings about the person we lost and we remain overly-involved with or unable to let go of that person. Without completing this grieving, we can be left with unconsciously trying to replace or correct for our loss each time we start a new adult relationship.

According to Psychoanalytic Theory, if our same-sex parent is missing from our home during childhood, it complicates the identification process necessary for resolving what is called the "Oedipus" or the "Electra" complex, and we're left unable to transfer our love from our opposite-sex parent to an appropriate partner as an adult. Since no one was there to "compete" with us for the affection of this opposite-sex parent, we've never been able to appropriately resolve the relationship, then go on to identify with our same-sex parent, and progress from there. One study showed that when a man grew up without a father in his home, he was more likely to have a lot of dating activity, but much less likely to actually ever get engaged or married.

Relationship Development

In addition to those internal and external influences that affect our relationships, there are other challenges along the road that will determine our success or failure. We have to be able to establish trust and then navigate through the developmental steps in a progression, advancing through the various stages of a relationship.

ESTABLISHING TRUST

Rather than believing you can't trust men ... women can be encouraged to proceed slowly. Instead of plunging ahead with impulsive abandon, they can size a lover up and put him to the test of time. Is he loyal? How does he treat his family and friends? Is he kind to those who are defenseless and unfortunate?

W. S. Appleton, 1981,
Fathers and Daughters, p. 130-131

Trust develops slowly through communicating, observing the other's actions, and learning to recognize and accept the partner's own unique way of showing that they are trustworthy. Some of us find it difficult to express our feelings freely, but we can show how we feel in other ways. Some of us find it hard to speak our thoughts very clearly, but we can explain something beautifully in writing. Some are afraid of being pressured or harshly judged, but will expose more of ourselves if we have a chance to test it slowly and watch our partner's reactions. Within the right context, most of us want to share our thoughts with someone special who will listen and understand. Rather than feeling reluctant to say anything at all for fear that the other person won't accept us or won't reciprocate, we can begin by cautiously saying something that is minimally threatening, observe their response, and then gradually, a little at a time, open up further, patiently, as trust slowly develops. It helps to be able to acknowledge the other ways in which we, and our partner, do reciprocate.

Being cautious during the early development of trust is also helpful in negotiating the complicated balancing act of trying to be open to getting to know someone new and at the same time trying to avoid letting the negative parts of some previous partnership contaminate the current one. In our relationships, as in most aspects of life, we need to let each new experience determine a new response – while still being able to incorporate our learning from the past.

We should be careful to get out of an
experience only the wisdom that is in it – and
stop there; lest we be like the cat that sits
down on a hot stove lid. She will never sit
We should be careful to get out of an
experience only the wisdom that is in it – and
stop there; lest we be like the cat that sits
down on a hot stove lid. She will never sit down on a hot
stove lid again – and that is well;
but also she will never sit down on a cold one.

Mark Twain (1800s)

THE PROGRESSION

"I'm always impatient to get to the middle of
a relationship. We've all been through too
many beginnings. I want to feel comfortable
with somebody, and would gladly give up the
excitement of the first few dates for the
opportunity to move on to the next stage."

Interview by William Novak, 1983,
The Great American Man Shortage, p. 94-95

The way that a relationship begins has an important impact on how it develops. Some theorists say that initial impressions and conditions continue to influence us in a relationship long after the conditions themselves no longer actually exist. On the other hand, many couples describe their initial meeting as completely uneventful, remembering being impressed only slightly or even not at all by a future partner. Either way, a lot can be understood about a relationship, especially the unconscious needs that we bring to it, when we describe our first meeting, our first impressions of each other, and what then (or later) attracted us to the other. Quite commonly, we describe a characteristic that first attracted us to a partner as the very same thing that later leaves us exasperated or dissatisfied. For example, we might initially be attracted to a person who makes us feel taken care of and secure, but later on this makes us feel controlled and over-protected. Or, maybe at the beginning, having opposite ways of coping with a problem seemed very interesting and attractive, but later on in the relationship we both start feeling annoyed, wondering how the other can possibly think the way they do.

There's also a tendency in the early part of a relationship to idealize the partner. Then we each attempt to perpetuate our partner's romanticized view of us by showing only those behaviors that are worthy of the idealization. But, since we want to try to be honest with one another, soon someone admits to being somewhat less wonderful than our partner makes us out to be, all the while hoping to hear a spirited denial that there was any such exaggeration. Hoping to have the partner continue the adoration....

Research evidence does find that it's important (maybe essential) to the success of a relationship to have some vision of the partner with "rose-colored glasses." It does help when we try to preserve some of our initial idealization. This is best achieved if we try to give each other credit for being responsible for the good things that happen in life and in the relationship, while we attribute the bad things to fate or circumstances. Our relationship is more likely to bloom with some amount of "accentuate the positive" and "eliminate the negative" (or at least overlook it).

Once a relationship is established, couples tend to lose some of the non-verbal interaction that was initially taking place. Flirting no longer seems necessary. Courtship activity tends to be only temporary. Men are particularly known for their "courtship and capture" phase, during which they're charming, thoughtful, sensitive – and then forget this behavior as their feelings change to a comfortable sense of closeness. Women tend to misinterpret this change. They still want the initial courting and romance, even though the diminishing of it might actually be a sign of trust and belief in the relationship.

When a healthy relationship progresses, intimacy and interdependence grow, and our fears about vulnerability decrease as we spend more time together and commitment grows. As involvement deepens, the benefits of the relationship become more and more available to both partners. We have new opportunities to enjoy and to appreciate the activities and interests of our partner, while we still continue our own pursuits, and while we're also seeking new ventures and adventures together. We each learn to accept the other's strengths as well as peculiarities, and we accommodate each other in a way that leaves neither of us feeling compromised or diminished but rather valuing both our new connections and our partner's unique ways and ideas.

In a survey of couples who were either married or had been living together for at least ten years, and where both partners described their relationship as successful and happy, one interesting finding was that neither of them saw themselves as ever having to make compromises in their relationship. Since we know that, actually, relationships do always involve compromise, this probably means that what other people might describe as having to make concessions, these successful couples saw as cooperation. They saw the wishes and needs of their partner, even when they were different from their own, as something that they were happy to be able to fulfill.

One married couple decided to move to a new location in a new climate, far away from what the woman thought of as her "home." She was having some difficulty adjusting, especially to the difference in the weather. She really missed the rain. She loved the calming sound of rainfall on the roof. After some time had passed, she went back to visit a friend in the old neighborhood and her husband stayed home to finish up some projects. She returned to a wonderful surprise that he had waiting for her. He was planning it before she went away, and managed to finish the whole thing while she was gone so it was ready when she came back. He had added a glass sunroom

onto one side of the house — and then installed a sprinkler system up on the roof so that she could turn it on whenever she wanted to hear the sound of rain!

THE STAGES OF DEVELOPMENT

Some theorists describe the unfolding of a relationship similarly to the stages of development that we see in a child. Based on this, they predict that the more optimally the falling in love stage progresses (the bonding), the more smoothly we will be able to navigate through the crucial developmental transitions in the growing romance. It also helps, of course, when both partners have had a good initial bonding experience in our own childhood.

In the first stage of the relationship, bonding, both partners are madly in love and the relationship is characterized by idealization, a lack of boundaries, a magical sense of knowing exactly what the other person is thinking or feeling, and a focus on similarities (often dramatically exaggerated — "WOW! You mean you like caramel ice cream, too?"). This is generally the first six to nine months of involvement.

After this intense period, comes an individuation phase, when one of us becomes ready to turn our energy toward the outside world. We ask for some separate free time, maybe even appearing to be selfish and stubborn about it (similar to the toddler who is beginning to seek independence). Tension may result if we aren't in the same phase of the developing relationship. If one of us still wants to be in the bonding phase, change can provoke fear of separation and abandonment. The one who is ready for the next stage may find this smothering. But, if we can instead be reassuring about our love and commitment, the transition can still proceed successfully.

In the third stage, we both usually become more emotionally disengaged from one another and might typically get involved in power and control battles (just as we see with adolescents). On the surface, our arguments seem to focus on specific daily life issues (this is the "right" way to load the dishwasher; this is the "best" way to pay the bills) but often the battles really are about some unconscious unmet childhood need that we were hoping the other would be able to satisfy. This challenging stage usually makes both of us feel that compromise is much more like surrender than cooperation!

Hopefully we survive this transition and reach the fourth phase, in which we are genuinely able to experience that we are staying in the relationship out of choice rather than out of need. During this stage, conflicts actually <u>are</u> about current issues, and not childhood leftovers, and we have developed, or are developing, new ways to handle the conflicts. We take responsibility for ourselves without blaming the other; we are able to support rather than undermine the success of the other; we share the power instead of struggling for it; and we aren't afraid of showing our insecurities to one another. At this stage, we are able to handle both closeness and distance without it being a threat to the relationship.

The final stage is one in which there is a natural urge to want to create something together or else to commit to something outside of the relationship, maybe to include a child, or to build a home together, or to engage in some charitable or political activities. This stage is characterized by extending the relationship boundaries, by appreciation of each other's differences rather than feeling frustrated by them, and by the strong bond that results from surviving all of the disillusionments of the earlier stages.

Someone who had been flying as a military pilot for many years described a similarity between a good relationship and flying in formation (although he associated this with birds rather than his fellow pilots!). One of the birds, he said, flies out in the front, leading the way, taking on the brunt of the oncoming turbulence, smoothing the air, and gracefully sheltering those who are following behind him. Instinctively (for birds, that is) the others know they can follow in a calm pathway, trusting the direction, realizing they are being protected along their route. After a while the lead flyer (I mean, bird) drops back, trading places with the next in formation. And then that one becomes the leader and the shield.

A swimmer also described the similarity between being in a relationship and the experience of sharing a swimming pool with other swimmers. Some of them splash, thrash, and churn the water so much that it adds to the struggle to move forward (or to the challenge, depending on how you look at it), while others just move smoothly through the water like dolphins, offering companionship without much disruption.

Chapter Ten

Love, Sex,
And Intimacy

Love

**My chief occupation, despite
appearances, has always been love.
I have a romantic soul, and have
always had considerable trouble
interesting it in something else.**

Albert Camus, <u>Notebooks 1942-1951</u>, p. 235

MANY PSYCHIATRISTS, PSYCHOLOGISTS, and psychotherapists — not to mention poets, writers, philosophers, composers, singers, artists, clergyman, and, well, almost everybody — have tried to describe and define love. According to Eric Fromm, a mature love is "a union under the condition of preserving one's integrity;" being united with our partner while still maintaining our individuality. According to Alfred Adler, the best love that we can achieve is giving and receiving unconditional love, knowing that regardless of any kind of disagreement or disapproval of our behavior, our love can be counted on to continue. According to Abraham Maslow, there is one love that comes from security or survival needs while another comes from higher needs like self-actualization. According to Sigmund Freud, one essential measure of good mental health is our ability to love.

There is love characterized by finding someone whose appearance correlates to an image that we hold in our mind, consciously or unconsciously. There is dramatic love that's about emotional intensity, obsession, or jealousy. There is fun love that's playful with childlike enjoyment. There is peaceful love that develops slowly with affection and companionship. There is practical love when the attributes or qualities of the loved one are consistent with what we want to achieve in our life. And, there is altruistic love when feelings of compassion or allegiance call for loving without expecting reciprocation.

Sometimes love is about fulfilling dependency needs; sometimes it's about feeling exclusive, absorbed in one another; sometimes it's about feeling an exhilarating physical passion. Or it could be about idealizing the partner, about wanting to help them, about being willing to sacrifice for them in their time of need. Some say that love's intensity can be measured by the sympathetic experience of pain when the loved one is in pain, or by the vicarious experience of stage fright when the loved one is performing. Some say it's about having trust, closeness, loyalty, respect, appreciation, sharing, accepting without criticism, having a true knowledge and deep understanding of the other. And some say the ingredients of love are simply friendship, commitment, and intellectual compatibility.

On the other hand ... love is also described as a disease, madness, a neurosis, a regression, an addiction, a curse, a plague! It's blamed for unpleasantness from head to toe: dizziness and lightheadedness, a lump in our throat, a pounding heart, butterflies in our stomach, sweaty palms, weak knees, cold feet. To add to all of these maladies, researchers have shown that when romantically involved couples try cooperative tasks involving business transactions, they don't perform nearly as well as two people who are not in love. When we're in love, we're less likely to come up with mutually beneficial ideas for negotiating deals and we're less likely to use any kind of pressure tactics. We might be able to communicate well with our partner about how to set our priorities and how to make a profit, but actual outcomes have us making less profit than our non-romantically involved competitors. So ... one cannot live on love alone....

Some stages of love are associated with discomfort, including fears, uncertainty, the feeling of being challenged, or the need to be reassured about the faithfulness and love of our partner. Since trust is difficult to achieve, we often experience pivoting back and forth between testing the other person's love in order to get reassurance, while, at the same time, feeling angry and confined by the "imprisonment" of our love. Then, as we become more and more involved, our expectations and demands increase, and our reactions become more negative (hostility, contempt, criticalness) if these expectations are not met.

Studies have shown that those of us who tend to fall in love easily hold the belief that love is ephemeral and that it is sex and chemistry that are the most important criteria in making a relationship endure. Those who have this "love prone" behavior were found to be less happy in love relationships and more likely to have had some traumatic or disruptive events in our childhood. Those who were identified as being the least love prone were more likely to describe another component as the most important thing in a relationship: trust.

Research also shows that men tend to be more romantic and to fall in love earlier in a relationship than do women. Men are both more idealistic and more cynical about love than women are, and more likely than women to fall into unrequited love. Women tend to have higher expectations about developing interpersonal intimacy and so they are more likely to be disappointed in what may end up being the reality of a relationship. They're usually more pragmatic than men about falling in love (maybe this is why they're slower to do so), but once they feel secure, they express their love more than men do.

Sex

Boy meets girl. Girl meets boy. Both are highly suspicious and even paranoid about the other person. Copulation replaces communication. Sex replaces love. The quest lasts about three milliseconds,

maybe three hours, and a kind of mutual
masturbation occurs, leaving both people
convinced that the old myths are dead.
The man believes no woman exists who can
give his life meaning. The woman feels no
prince will ever come along to discover the
princess within her. Both go away from
their sexual encounter throbbing and
feeling the words from the Rolling Stones'
hit song: "I can't get no satisfaction!"

Pierre Mornell, 1979,
Passive Men, Wild Women, p. 119-120

Women who were raised with the value of virginity (or, at least, the importance
of selective discrimination), but who have lived through the changing standards of
recent decades, have usually experienced a lot of conflict about sex. If a woman
believed that sexual intimacy should go together with romantic involvement and
commitment, then the pressure to engage quickly in sexual activity with someone
new would lead to hurt and disappointment if no further relationship actually
developed. A woman was expecting a growing attachment to a man with whom she
had sex, while a man was sometimes feeling just the opposite. A man seduced,
and, when the excitement of the conquest was over, he often lost interest.

From the biological perspective, as it relates to mammals, males can be
much less discriminating sexually than females because of the different investment
involved. In a cost-benefit analysis, the male just contributes one ejaculation
and it's to his benefit to spread his seed around to reproduce as many offspring
as possible. The "cost" to the female, though, is much more complicated. It
includes impregnation, gestation, lactation, weaning, and, for most species, post-
weaning responsibilities. The best sexual strategy from this perspective involves
the female's ability to resist unless she thinks the male is especially suitable for
reproduction. She is limited in how often she can reproduce, so she needs to
optimize the chances that her offspring will survive and prosper.

Today, with modern birth control methods, most people feel that we're no longer so concerned about this as a consequence of having sex (although women still carry the main burden of an unanticipated pregnancy). It used to be that men complained about women holding back or lacking sexual responsiveness, but, after the "sexual revolution," many men admitted that they found women's new expectations to be intimidating. They worried about their own ability to satisfy a woman. One significant negative change as a result of women's liberation was a great increase in reports of male impotence.

The importance of sexual satisfaction in a relationship cannot be underestimated and some researchers have found that this makes or breaks the quality and stability of a marriage. However, with early pressure to "perform," often before we're really ready to even be involved with each other, sexual interaction can become much more complicated and problematic than we think. In spite of cultural changes that made this easier in some ways, for many women and men, one of the troublesome parts of establishing a healthy sexual relationship is the negative effect of some inappropriate or abusive childhood or adolescent experience. The after effects of this can make it much more difficult to trust in the early part of a relationship.

So I grew up mistrusting "nice men" as much as those men who did, in fact, try to molest me, grew up imagining that anyone who came within a foot of me was about to attack me, grew up feeling, alongside of my positive sexual drive, recurrent surges of disgust toward all forms of sexuality whatsoever.

**Ingrid Bengis, 1972,
Combat in the Erogenous Zone, p. 13**

Intimacy

Intimacy, although often confused with sex, is not the same as sex. It's possible to have sex without intimacy and it's possible to have intimacy without sex

— although it's the combination of the two that poets and authors often write about. The sharing of an intimate moment or an intimate discussion can sometimes be experienced with a stranger, but the achievement of real intimacy in a relationship, just like the development of trust, is a process, something that happens over time. It is characterized by intense feelings at times, sharing very personal things, respecting commitments, feeling mutually accepted, feeling a positive sense of self-esteem, being able to resolve conflicts together, sharing resources, and identifying the relationship using the term "we" rather than "you" and "I." It's giving moral support and encouragement to each other, being interested in whatever is going on in the other's life, doing chores or favors for the other, offering material help or support if it's needed, giving gifts, giving verbal and physical expressions of love and affection, and being willing to tolerate some of the partner's less pleasant aspects. We expose things about ourselves that we usually keep private: our history, values, hopes, fears, strengths, weaknesses, idiosyncrasies. We focus on compatibility, our similarities, and on the reciprocity in our relationship.

Intimacy is when we share our thoughts and feelings, not out of dependency, but out of a desire to really deeply know about someone else's life, and a sense that we can truly share our own life. This is most likely to develop when the relationship produces a sense of harmony and positive feelings. When it promotes growth and allows surrender of some control to the other. When it encourages communicating and expressing care or concern. When it overcomes limitations of time and space (they exist but don't get in the way). When it lets us escape from the outside world into our own corner and at the same time gives us a sense of connection to the outside world from within our partnership.

This is a concept that is not easy to measure. What one person considers a close confidant might just be a casual acquaintance to another. Many of our cultural changes have challenged traditionally accepted ideas of sexuality, exclusivity, commitment, and permanence. Defining the parameters of an intimate relationship has to be determined by the individuals. Perhaps part of the development of intimacy is in this definition.

According to developmental theorists, those of us who are high in intimacy long for closeness and contact but are balanced by the wish for autonomy and independent functioning. We might have mild anxiety about attachments but we're able to have deep relationships with male and female friends as well as get involved in committed romantic relationships. Those of us who are at a middle level of intimacy have deep relationships with friends but are still ambivalent about romantic commitment. Those of us who would be considered low in intimacy might be completely withdrawn or else have relationships, even enduring committed ones, but with only superficial involvement and lacking any real depth or closeness. This group has strong anxieties about attachment and separation, both, and will often tend to feel depressed.

Another group are those of us who are considered to be <u>overly</u> intimate. That is, we have relationships (really entanglements), sometimes even committed ones, that are based on dependency and our need to be completely immersed without any boundaries or distinctions between the others and ourselves. We tend to argue and bicker, perhaps fighting against our own inclination to be too immersed while trying to protect ourselves from our dread of separation. We also struggle with anxiety and depression.

There are also some of us who are described as having high intimacy motivation. This is a readiness for a certain kind of interpersonal experience that makes us receptive to warm, close, and communicative interactions. We're not necessarily pursuing friendship or activities with other people. Instead, we're just sensitive and open to having intimacy in our daily life. Our emphasis is on allowing ourselves to experience the intimacy that is already there, not in trying to attain it. Being able to do this is associated with allowing a loosening of the usually accepted boundaries between people, probably surrendering a little of the control, and being open to the spontaneous things that happen rather than focusing on some specific activity.

Those who are high in intimacy motivation have more one-to-one close friendship interactions, more personal discussions with people, do more listening, have concern for the well-being of others, can accept close physical proximity, and express more positive feelings in interactions with others. Our friends and acquaintances usually see us being warmer, more natural, sincere, loving, and appreciative, while less dominant, outspoken, and self-centered than those of us who are low in intimacy motivation. This is a quality that is positively associated with healthy psychosocial adjustment. Research shows that having high intimacy motivation predicts success in our relationships, occupation, and overall mental health.

... intimacy, that is, the capacity to commit himself to concrete affiliations and partnerships and to develop the ethical strength to abide by such commitments, even though they may call for significant sacrifices and compromises.

Erik Erikson, 1963, <u>Childhood and Society</u>, p. 263

CHAPTER ELEVEN

Commitment

**Human relations are problematic
because men are driven by opposing but
often equally powerful needs and
passions, especially the needs for
security and freedom. To satisfy the
need for security, people seek
closeness and commitment, and the more
they attain these, the more oppressed
they feel. To satisfy their need for
freedom, people seek independence and
detachment, and the more they attain
these, the more isolated they feel. As in
all such things, the wise pursue the
golden mean; and the lucky attain it.**

Unknown

MAINTAINING A RELATIONSHIP requires work: problem solving, self-disclosing, making attempts to change our troublesome behavior. When we actually make a commitment to a partner, as well as strengthening our feelings of love, it also increases how much effort we're willing to put out in order to do that work. Although we usually have ambivalence in some form from the very beginning of dating someone, once we make the commitment, our doubt decreases. Before the commitment is made, there is sometimes an increase in conflict or negativity, but once we pledge our loyalty, this subsides. There are disputes still, but they are no longer related to whether or not to continue the relationship. Now they're about the actual issues that are getting in the way of compatibility. We no longer see things as being either all good or all bad because we no longer feel that we have to make a decision about the relationship. Now we can more easily look at and work on the things that need improvement. Also, just being committed to sharing life together rather than to being together because we're "in love," helps us transcend those moments when, inevitably, we'll be feeling like we don't even like each other....

As we continue to invest in the relationship (our time, our energy, our resources), we experience more and more commitment. Even if there are times when our investment starts feeling like it's greater than the "exchange" seems to be worth, our feelings about the commitment that we've made keeps us there. It might also be stirring up some sense of entrapment, but the key ingredient seems to be the element of choice. When we feel that we've really chosen freely to invest ourselves in a particular way, then dealing with some of the imbalances and some giving up of other things, results in strengthening our feelings of commitment even further.

Some studies have shown that those who tend to make commitments early in life, like choosing to "go steady," often are higher in self-esteem, give marriage higher value, feel more sure about marrying, expect to marry sooner, and are less willing to stay single than the young people who haven't chosen steady relationships. These observations are based on a very young population, though, so they probably don't account for people who are focused on achievements in other areas during these early years but who will still go on later to make mature relationship commitments.

It's also important to note that, for some, what looks like an apparent resistance to commitment might just be a thin veneer of caution, before actually taking the plunge.

Marriage Concepts

In an English comedy written by William Congreve in 1693, one of the characters stated: "Courtship is to marriage as a very witty prologue is to a very dull play." Maybe even then, just as now, couples must have struggled to achieve some balance between dependence and independence, devotion and separateness, security and excitement.

By 1947 (two and a half centuries later!), the concept of the "liberated marriage" had begun to emerge. The husband should be older and should "wear the pants" in the family. The wife should be fully informed about family finances and can manage some of the money on her own, including having a household budget and maybe a small personal budget. The husband should have an active part in disciplining and training the children. The husband and wife should take vacations together, should have shared standards of sexual morality, and should express their love to one another often.

Over the next few decades, however, this concept became less clear-cut. One theorist proposed that there are four stages of development, philosophically, in the way we think about marriage. At first we have "magical beliefs," including the fairy-tale views where there are no flaws and where emotional reasoning will conquer all. With this type of thinking, conflict of any kind is considered a threat to the relationship. In the second stage, we have "idealized conventional views," including the unconditional acceptance of many socially approved ideas, such as partners should work on things together, share in responsibilities, and cooperatively solve problems about the relationship itself as well as things like finances or illness.

With the third stage emerges an "individualistic concept," which allows each of us to have our own preferences and needs. This allows us to focus on our personal growth while still encouraging what is needed to continue to strengthen the relationship. In the last stage, we have an "affirmational belief" system in which we are able to acknowledge and cope with the inevitable conflicts that are bound to arise in a marriage. We accept that beliefs, values, and emotions change over time, so therefore, conflicts are bound to happen and will need to be resolved. In this stage, we understand that being flexible is a necessary ingredient in order to handle ambiguities.

A couple decided to make a real commitment to resolving their differences, first by talking about them in therapy sessions and then by adding their own private meetings at home. So every Thursday evening became the "family ritual" of sitting down in the same specific place, at the same particular time, with something comforting to drink (a cup of tea or hot chocolate or a glass of wine – but only one), to discuss various issues that had taken place during the week. First they brought up important things that happened during their separate time, sharing their most positive and most negative experience of the week as well as anything that they were worried about or that they wanted to hear their partner's opinion about. Then they talked about their week with respect to each other, including giving compliments and praise, making requests for change, bringing up things they thought might have been misunderstandings, and discussing any future plans they had in mind. When the topic was difficult, they used the technique of paraphrasing the partner first and then responding with their own side of the story. When it was particularly heated or emotional, they used a technique of holding some kind of a "sacred object" (like a "talking stick"), where only the one holding it speaks. When that person finishes talking (no filibustering!), they pass the object to the other, who first paraphrases and then gives their perspective. Just their commitment to using these techniques changed the whole tone of their relationship. Knowing that they would soon have a chance to talk over any issues, their frustrations and resentments subsided. Hope had a chance to grow as they saw their success at resolving issues, and they began to look forward to their new ritual, occasionally talking late into the night about their plans and dreams.

Living Together

The social upheaval and changes in government that took place during the 1960s affected a wide range of people, perhaps especially those of us born during the time of the Baby Boomer generation. For many, it gave rise to deep feelings of insecurity about the meaning of permanence, and, as a result, uncertainty about the value of having only one exclusive relationship. One effect was that many of us were making commitments in a more limited way. Couples who decided to live together without marrying increased by 800% during the 60s. Although this was considered to be an alternative to marriage for many of us, for most it was actually just a new stage in courtship, often a very useful one. Making a commitment to live together added two new dimensions to a relationship, revealing many issues about interpersonal compatibility as well as ability to cooperate or be flexible within the realities of day-to-day living. The first new dimension was learning each other's eating habits, cleanliness, sexual compatibility, decision-making, ability and willingness to assume responsibility, and the ability of one partner to take charge and be stable and protective if the other one was ill or under stress. The second new dimension was the ability of the partners to adapt to the outside world as a couple, having to meet the demands of society and social situations, and having to handle the restrictions that are involved in being part of a partnership.

A woman met a man at a ski resort where they thoroughly enjoyed the outdoor adventure during the day and then sitting and talking quietly by the fireside in the evening. They lived in far-away different states, so they made a plan to meet again to share another "adventure" – and then another and another. They went rafting, kayaking, hiking, rock climbing, as well as finding less challenging activities like going to a ball game, a rock concert, the racetrack. They were having a great time and she began thinking of him as the "King of the Mountain" because he always seemed to know his way around, no matter where they were or what they were doing. Then he told her his job contract at home was ending (not unexpectedly) and they decided that he would

take some time off and spend a month living with her before he looked for another job. Finances weren't really a problem for either of them, but they decided that she would continue paying the usual expenses of living in her home and he would pay for their food, entertainment, and transportation. That part of it worked out well. But that was the only thing. By the end of the second week, he was looking at her blankly, sure that she was from a different planet, and she was looking mystified at him, thinking that he must be a runaway from the outback. He might have been king of the mountain, but he was a misfit in the city. And he certainly didn't fit into this castle. They had a wonderful time doing things together, but as "dance" partners in everyday life, they both had two left feet! Sad but accepting, they laughed and talked about it, and then spent the rest of the month happily knowing that he'd move again at the end of it.

Many couples who live together do go on to get married. Sometimes they change the traditional commitment vows. Just as a promise to "obey" was changed to a promise to "cherish" in most marriage ceremonies, some also changed the vows from "as long as we both shall live" to "as long as we both shall love." Perhaps for some of us this made commitments more tolerable, but it has also been said that it might be that this loophole contributed to some people never being able to fully blossom within a marriage, lacking the security of that enduring promise of "till death do us part."

Alignment of purpose is the condition out of which powerful love relationships are formed. It has nothing to do with likes or dislikes, how good looking they are, or music, books, perfume, or any of that stuff you thought it did.

**Ron Smotherman, 1980,
<u>Winning Through Enlightenment</u>, p. 132-133**

CHAPTER TWELVE

Roadblocks and Barriers

SO WHY ARE SO many of us failing to establish enduring intimate relationships in spite of proclaiming a wish for this? Some of us can't handle the discrepancy between our own expectations and the actual realities of day-to-day relationships. Some get into relationships where both partners need nurturing but neither is capable of doing the nurturing. Some are struggling to balance our desire for intimacy and commitment with our fear of loss of privacy and freedom.

Some of the common roadblocks include our own expectations, our unresolved issues of separation from our parents, our narcissism and perfectionism, our traumatic life experiences including exposure to sexual abuse, and our fears related to loss.

Expectations

> **Expectation is the enemy of intimacy. The more a man feels pressured to live up to a woman's expectations, the less likely he is to relax and open up. Men, like women, want to be accepted for who they are, rather than be expected to become what someone else wants or needs them to be.**
>
> **Cowan and Kinder, 1985,**
> **Smart Women, Foolish Choices, pp. 201-202**

Our fantasies about romance and fulfillment can accompany us on a date and the potential partner can often sense this unconsciously. Having specific role expectations can have a similar effect. For example, a woman who wants a strong and confident man might not be able to allow him to express his insecurities or his fears without judging him. Maybe the transition away from traditional sex role expectations in our culture cleared up some problems while creating new ones. It was liberating for many of us to be able to be "who we are," but it also left many things ambiguous and confusing. What is still clear, though, is that the greater the number of specific expectations that we have when we go into a relationship, the less likely that the relationship will be able to succeed because of the loss of one of the most essential ingredients for intimacy. That ingredient is having the ability to be open and self-revealing, without a need for masks or disguises.

On the other hand, some research has shown that having general expectations, if they are positive, is very helpful. Seeing a basic value and worth in other people; feeling that our partner can be trusted and won't betray our trust; assuming that he or she will be understanding and appreciative; believing that they really want to be committed to us and to love us; anticipating that they'll be sensitive, gentle, respectful, good, and caring. Having these expectations in our mind can actually improve our chances of getting these qualities in a relationship. They give a partner something to live up to by establishing a positive mindset, a mental model for conducting the partnership.

Unresolved Separation Issues

Those who don't have a firm sense of our own separateness or individuality can find the uniting experience of intimacy frightening because we fear a loss of our identity. We can find ourselves either repeatedly disappointed in relationships or else becoming isolated and self-absorbed. Or perhaps vacillating between the two.

A mature relationship requires that both partners feel secure and confident as separate individuals and able to encourage each other to maintain this individuality even while united as a couple. An immature relationship is likely to be based on unconscious needs to correct or compensate for something that wasn't satisfied in our childhood. It can be filled with fear of abandonment, conflict about dependence and independence, and ambiguity about closeness and distance. Until we've resolved our own issues about our individuality and separateness (either from our parents or the parent images that we hold unconsciously), it can be difficult to actually see a new partner clearly and accept their qualities without having some contamination from the past.

As we've discussed, a girl's childhood process of becoming independent usually involves first identifying with and then later separating from her parent of the same sex, her mother. As a result, as women we sometimes have difficulty establishing autonomy and boundaries in adult relationships. We function as if we aren't autonomous at all but are part of a unit that's being regulated almost entirely by the needs of the other (which is often the experience of being a mother, that person with whom we identified). But for many of us, this role eventually feels too confining. We might say we want intimacy with a man, but when we actually get it, we become uncomfortable and critical.

> **They blame it on something particular about the person – he's too smart or not smart enough; he's too short or too tall; he's too passive or too aggressive; he's too successful or not successful enough; he's too needy or seems too self-contained … how quickly a woman will rush for her checklist, how easily she will find ways to dismiss this person whose nearness is making her uneasy.**
>
> **Lillian Rubin, 1983, Intimate Strangers, p. 84-85**

Usually a boy has to first be able to separate from someone of the opposite sex, his mother, and then later on in life attach to another person of the opposite sex but in a completely different way. Because of this, a man might unconsciously resist closeness because he's afraid that he might once again become attached to the point of that deep dependency that he knew when he was a baby. Since he really wants to connect in spite of his resistance, he might meanwhile be left wondering why deep down inside he has this uneasy feeling that he can't trust women....

He moves close, wanting to share some part of himself with her, trying to do so, perhaps even yearning to experience again the bliss of the infant's connection with a woman. She responds, female style – wanting to touch him just a little more deeply, to know what he's thinking, feeling, fearing, wanting. And the fear closes in – the fear of finding himself again in the grip of a powerful woman, of allowing her admittance only to be betrayed and abandoned once again, of being overwhelmed by denied desires.

Lillian Rubin, 1983, Intimate Strangers, p. 83

Narcissism

Some have said that we live in an age of selfishness and an epidemic of narcissism has created a society of "princes" and "princesses." The Baby Boomers were the first generation in American history in which most children were raised in relative affluence. Many of us learned to expect that goals could be achieved with little delay or frustration rather than with the patience, luck, and compromise that really are necessary for things like long-term relationships.

Often loneliness went along with this kind of affluence. Maybe our parents were so busy working, building a life of prosperity for us, that they didn't have time to enjoy it with us. And some of us didn't have the necessity to earn any money and so missed out on the value of working, missed out on the chance to be proud of our accomplishments. Or we had parents who went overboard with constantly praising us for things, leaving us with the expectation that others will also do this in the "real" world. Those who didn't learn the <u>genuine</u> feelings of success and failure, pride in what we are able to accomplish and acceptance of what we don't do well, are left more vulnerable to being crushed both by peer pressure and by reality, more vulnerable than those of us who did struggle with some sense of day-to-day survival.

So, some of us may have grown up not wanting to make any room in our lives for personal commitment. If we felt we had to remain emotionally self-protective, we might have focused just on personal growth even though we might have wanted closeness. If we didn't have any appropriate intimacy in our early life, we spent our energy, sometimes indiscriminately, looking for feedback that we <u>are</u> actually lovable. Then we would thrive on being told we are handsome or beautiful, that others are in love with us, that we are really unique and wonderful. Maybe we could learn to inspire romantic love in others but were incapable of actually being able to feel it ourselves, so we substituted a variety of partners for any true depth of feelings. We could enjoy the excitement and dramatic thrill of the beginning of a relationship: a narcissistic man sweeps a woman off her feet, overwhelming her with attention and passion. She finds him captivating. Although she senses something isn't quite right, she still responds with her own narcissism, wanting to believe that she truly is "special." But it doesn't last. We're "in love with love" but we're afraid of the real thing. So we're left feeling inauthentic, unable to fill our hunger for the excitement of romance, the excitement that hides us from our inner sense of emptiness. Once again, we manage to avoid any danger of feeling dependency, but simultaneously craving and yet dreading intimacy.

One woman was very focused on showing a man that she was exceptional and wonderful and that he would be very lucky to have her in his life. She excelled in many things already, but she learned some of the hobbies and sports that he was interested in and quickly became as good as he was at them. And he <u>was</u> indeed dazzled! Then a day came when she was truly in need of his help and support. She had been injured in an accident and she was feeling very exhausted and extremely vulnerable.

He didn't have the slightest idea how to relate to this part of her, a part that he'd never seen before, and nothing that he did felt right. She was left feeling very alone in her pain, though she knew he was trying to be helpful to her. She thought that she had to be extraordinary at all times in order to be lovable. But, of course, then she couldn't really feel loved because that was only one part of her, the part of her for "show," not the authentic whole person with fears and needs and vulnerabilities.

Perhaps this roadblock is being more concerned with wanting a partner to think that we are wonderful rather than in finding out how wonderful they are, and really, who they are. It seems that the flawed premise is in using the Golden Rule: that we should do unto others as we would have them do unto us. Loving someone else isn't about treating them the way that we would want to be treated. That might be true with some things, but the more difficult part is learning how to treat them in the way that they would want to be treated. For example, if it's their birthday, do we give them a weekend at a place that we know they would love? Or do we give them a tent because we think it would be fun to go camping? The gift of the tent can be nice because it is something about our own life that we want to share with them and that can be special. But if what they want is to go to a lodge at the seashore … well, it is their birthday. Maybe we should give them the tent when it's our birthday. The Relationship Golden Rule says "Do unto others as they would have us do unto them."

Idealism and Perfectionism

One couple went to a store where they make bedding so that the man could get a feather pillow made for himself. He was excited to take the custom pillow home and try it out, but the next morning he told his wife that he thought it was too firm. So, she took it back to the store and the lady there agreeably removed some of the feathers. He

tried it out again, but the next morning he said it was now too soft. Once again his wife returned to the store and explained the problem. The nice saleslady, while she was restoring some of the feathers, looked at her and said, knowingly, "Tonight you give your husband a rock to sleep on and tomorrow he will be happy with the pillow!"

Many theorists agree that perfectionism probably develops from being raised in an environment of either non-approval or inconsistent approval (never feeling able to please our parents), or else in an environment of conditional approval (pleasing them only when things are done "right" – that is, their way). Since we need to feel loved and accepted, we are motivated to keep on striving, seeking perfection, but the feelings of insecurity and uncertainty that come from this type of parenting keep us from feeling that we've ever actually been able to achieve our goal or even that we deserve it. Still we keep on trying.

The traits that then commonly develop include polarized thinking (we see things as either black or white, all or nothing), over-generalizing (we think in terms of "always" or "never"), and a very moralistic self-evaluation based on how we think we "should" be. Unrealistically high expectations leave us feeling frustrated and unlovable, often lonely, so even if something is accomplished successfully, those of us who are perfectionists are not likely to be able to really enjoy our accomplishment.

In relationships, perfectionists have difficulty because we are anticipating failing when we, inevitably, can't meet up to our own standards. We're also hypersensitive to criticism from others, which can make us withdraw from close social involvements. Since our defensive reaction to criticism often alienates others, this then reinforces our belief that we must be perfect for acceptance. The fear of being seen as inadequate also can make us reluctant to disclose things about ourselves, so we stay safe, but meanwhile we sabotage getting the closeness that we really want.

We probably apply our overly perfectionistic standards to others as well, making it even more difficult to find our "ideal" partner. In order to attract that desired partner, we must have enough to offer in the "marketplace" to make the exchange equitable. Not being chosen is because of not having sufficient assets. As self-critical perfectionists, our feelings of low self-esteem become our biggest barrier to starting and then keeping a successful relationship. We want our ideal partner but we don't feel we are worthy of him or her. Even if we find someone, we don't feel adequate enough to deserve or sustain it.

A man was trying to reconcile his fears of loneliness with his inability to accept what he saw as "flaws" in others. He understood intellectually that some concerns weren't really important, even to him. There was no "right" way to wear a scarf, or to hang a towel in the bathroom, or to talk on the telephone, or to read a paper. But he wasn't able to let things go. In his mind the right partner would know how to do these things in the same way that he did. Meanwhile, he continued to cross people off of his list of possible partners for the slightest reason. Then he met someone who was even more perfectionistic than he was. Suddenly he saw his own behavior in a "mirror" and it was very startling to him. He hadn't been able to see this in himself, but he could clearly see this other person hiding from the insecurity of being imperfect and fear of being rejected because of it. Overcoming this was not easy for him. It helped to realize that he was doing to others the same thing his parents had done to him. He started by relearning a few childhood things – this time imperfectly. He colored outside the lines, spilled some coffee on his shirt, walked through a big mud puddle, played a game that he wasn't good at, started to make something and didn't finish it – all the while smiling to himself! Then he started translating this acceptance of himself to others, learning to let it be okay for others to do things their own way, differently than he would, even imperfectly....

Even having a mental expectation of finding an ideal mate can be self-defeating in itself. The more someone feels pressured to be ideal or to be someone else's notion of ideal, the less likely that a close relationship can actually develop since, once again, the crucial elements of being self-revealing and accepting are likely to be blocked.

But ... are these personality traits really a major cause of relationship problems?

But it isn't, as some critics have charged, simply selfishness, immaturity, narcissism, or some other newly discovered and widespread character flaw that makes binding commitments so difficult in the present era. To write such major social changes off with an analysis that focuses on personal psychopathology is to trivialize the impact of the social world on the lives of the people who live in it and to elevate psychology to a cause of our social malaise rather than an effect of it.

Lillian Rubin, 1983, Intimate Strangers, p. 4

Our culture now seems to emphasize changing partners when we are dissatisfied rather than on resolving problems, adding to the difficulty of learning how to sustain our relationships. The inevitable flaws in real life relationships are disillusioning when movies and television give us the impression that romantically speedy solutions to real problems are the norm. Our society is also promoting our unrealistic expectations because of the importance placed on physical attractiveness. Since we attribute other positive qualities as well to people who are attractive, appearance becomes a high priority in the sense of having made a good "bargain" in the marketplace of love. With so much exposure to the media and celebrities, we are encouraged to have unreasonably high standards, and are then perhaps disappointed with those who are actually available to us.

Traumatic Life Experiences

According to the medical concept, "trauma" is a severe emotional shock following a deeply distressing event or a serious physical injury. The shock will vary in the amount of impact that the event may potentially have on our life. If we end up having symptoms of post-traumatic stress disorder (PTSD), it has been said that our "protective psychic shield" has been overrun by an event that is too overwhelming for our mind to master or regulate. We haven't been able to do the necessary mental processing, so we're left with our thoughts, feelings, and memories stuck, continuing to occupy a place in our mind's everyday functioning. Since remembering may be unbearable, repression ("forgetting") is highly likely, which then produces a cycle that alternates between being emotionally numb, or in complete denial, to suddenly having an unanticipated triggering of thoughts that are frightening and that we associate with the incident.

Most theorists agree that the after-effects of traumatic events include emotional numbing, withdrawal, and problems with intimacy. Some say the trauma of early loss (or dysfunctional family relationships) results in limiting someone's potential for forming attachments altogether, maybe even leading to resentment that confusingly co-exists in conflict with a yearning for love and support.

Much of the intervention in psychotherapy is related to trying to uncover deeply repressed traumatic events, or to deal with current ones, by consciously remembering and re-experiencing the event in a more adaptive way, relieving the confusion, the panic, and the avoidance that the event may have produced. There are two separate schools of thought about what determines the extent of the impact we are likely to experience from a traumatic event. One focuses on the nature of the incident itself and the other emphasizes the particular make-up and thus response of a victim of the incident. Both of these are important in understanding the long-term effects that can occur in our life and relationships.

The "life events" school of thought led to the development of a rating scale of stressful experiences that was then used to establish our stress score. The literature about specific traumatic life events is extensive: victims of violence, rape, incest, sexual abuse, or severe psychological abuse; natural disasters; The Holocaust, the Vietnam War or other war experiences, being a hostage; having a miscarriage, still-birth, or abortion; divorce, widowhood, and many other life-changing events, whether negative or positive (even positive events can be traumatic). Later on, theorists also added daily "hassles" to the list, the small but aggravating events that occur frequently (and, all too often, on top of one another), thinking that these also can become as much a source of stress as major life events. As Freud had much earlier suggested:

It is not the latest slight – which in itself is minimal – that produces the fit of crying, the outburst of despair or the attempt at suicide, in disregard of the axiom that an effect must be proportionate to its cause; the small slight of the present moment has aroused and set working the memories of very many, more intense, earlier slights.

**Sigmund Freud and Josef Breuer, 1895,
Studies on Hysteria, p. 217**

This was the essence of the concept that later became known as "cumulative trauma," a series of accumulated stresses and strains that become disabling. Sometimes this happens all at once, sometimes over an extended period of time.

But considering these traumatic experiences only from the life events perspective had some limitations. One issue is that it's often difficult to isolate one specific event so that it is possible to prove that it was that particular trauma which was connected to our illness or dysfunctional behavior rather than any number of other possible causes. But a more important issue is that different individuals respond differently to the exact same or similar event, depending on our personality traits and background of experience. So, the second school of thought is that the impact of a traumatic event, including how it will affect our later relationships, depends not just on the particular event itself, but also on our own individual response to it.

Research on post-traumatic stress disorder has found that certain personalities are more prone to developing a psychological dysfunction after a trauma. For example, we are more vulnerable if we have a strong need to be in control of the environment, or if we were protected so much during our lifetime that we never developed an appropriate psychological "immunity" to danger.

Our response is also related to our developmental ability to understand what has happened and to see our responsibility in the situation. One study about children who personally witnessed the murder of one of their parents showed that younger children responded more easily to outside assistance because they were the most likely to feel helpless or passive in the traumatic situation. If the event occurred during adolescence, the teenager was more likely to feel somehow accountable for the outcome. Sometimes the event pushed them prematurely into a highly responsible adult role, but it also often sent them into self-destructive and acting-out behavior — trying to hide from the painful memories, or trying to assuage their feelings of guilt.

Sexual Abuse

One theorist described a model about childhood sexual abuse that differentiates the trauma into four factors: sexualization, betrayal, powerlessness, and stigmatization. The first factor, sexualization, results in dysfunctional sexual feelings and attitudes that are shaped by our childhood experience. Victims are likely to engage in inappropriate sexual behavior, generally with inappropriate partners. Usually we're confused about our own sexuality or we have highly exaggerated emotional reactions to any exposure to sexuality, whether personal or in the environment, even in the media.

The second is betrayal, which results when we realize that someone we looked up to, or were dependent on, has caused us harm. When we were also blamed, disbelieved, or even ostracized by others (including the abuser), the feelings of betrayal can be even worse. We can suffer a grief reaction, depression, or disillusionment with the breakdown of trust. We're sometimes left feeling extremely dependent, even on the abuser, while we painstakingly try to regain a sense of trust and security within ourselves. Or, it leaves us with poor judgment about the trustworthiness of others while we desperately look for some redeeming relationship to hold on to. And some of us will be pushed to exactly the opposite reaction – an aversion to any kind of intimacy at all.

The third factor is <u>powerlessness</u>. In this part of the dynamic as a trauma victim, our will seems to have been completely broken, our sense of effectiveness or usefulness in normal daily life seems seriously damaged. These feelings are even worse if the abuse is ongoing and our ability to stop it from happening has been continually defeated.

The fourth, <u>stigmatization</u>, is often really self-stigmatization because no one else may actually know about what happened. The abuse is now part of our self-image. We feel shame, guilt, or simply that we're somehow "bad" in an obscure uncomfortable way.

When we're unable to communicate about the abuse, especially if it is ongoing or violent, all of these issues become even further compounded. Perhaps we don't discuss the event because of our feelings of shame or because we're in complete denial. Maybe we're afraid someone's response will be disappointment or disapproval, anger or even rage. Or, frequently, maybe we've been threatened in a way that forces us to be silent. And sometimes it's even more complicated if the abuser was someone we loved and the fear of the loss of their love is still one more part of our agonizing dilemma.

Studies have shown that victims of childhood sexual abuse are more vulnerable to becoming involved in abusive relationships in adulthood. Also, other long-term effects include anxiety, guilt, low self-esteem, depression, social isolation, intimacy problems, promiscuity, sexual dysfunction, personal and sexual identity confusion, a tendency to sexualize relationships, and substance abuse. In a survey at a women's psychiatric clinic of patients who had a history of sexual abuse, the majority were found to be single, with more than a third having never been married. Besides physical abuse, sexual abuse, and rape, they had often also experienced having serious operations (including abortions), injuries, or multiple small accidents.

Some researchers have estimated that by the time we reach eighteen, as many as one third of women and at least one sixth of men have experienced an unwanted sexual encounter with an adult or an older adolescent male.

Fear Of Loss

Another reason that many of us block intimacy is because we're afraid of losing our identity, of being overly vulnerable, of being rejected or hurt, or of feeling foolish or inadequate. So we avoid closeness by not sharing our fears or hurt feelings or making any effort to reconcile our differences with a partner. Maybe it's easier to stay distant or accept defeat than to face the complications we're afraid of in intimate relationships.

Some theorists say that many who don't marry, or who don't stay married, suffer from "amoraphobia" — fear of a <u>successful</u> relationship. This could be, partially at least, a consequence of today's instant results culture. We get instant meals from a microwave oven, instant answers from a computer, instant relief from a pill, and we dream of instant wealth from a sweepstakes or lottery. Perhaps we think instant results should also be achieved in romantic relationships. But success in the form of "instant intimacy" actually often arouses our fear and mistrust. Suddenly we're close to someone who's really still a stranger, and then fear inhibits us from wanting to continue the slow growing process that's necessary to establish the true kind of intimacy that will remain stable over time.

Fears of loss generally fall into the following three categories with respect to our relationships: our fear of losing the other, our fear of losing our self, our fear of losing our freedom (limiting our options).

FEAR OF LOSING THE OTHER

Despite my firm belief in the importance of living "in the moment," every time I begin a relationship, I have to overcome my considerable sense of dread about the likelihood of its ending.

Ingrid Bengis, 1972,
<u>Combat in the Erogenous Zone</u>, p. 204-205

This describes the first type of fear of loss – the anticipation of <u>abandonment</u> or even death of the other person; of being rejected, hurt or disappointed; of becoming a failure in the relationship. Those of us with this type of fear usually want the support or belonging of a relationship and are engaged in pursuing it, trying to win the affection of others, but all the while we're anticipating what seems to be the inevitable ending before it even begins. Dating then becomes the approach-avoidance "dance," making an effort to be open and social while simultaneously being self-protective so as to avoid rejection. Some of this is in all of us. We're all aware that rejection is a possibility. But most of us can put it into perspective without having paralyzing thoughts about it.

Interestingly, observations that were made about attachment behavior in infants seem to parallel what happens to some of us in our adult romantic attachments. These observations showed that if an infant was removed from its mother for a period of time and then later reunited with her, the infant showed more separation anxiety than would normally be expected (from a heightened fear that the mother might leave again) or else an unusual sense of detachment, showing an apparent lack of interest in her. The infant seemed to go through three phases during the time of the separation. First it protested in every way that it could, trying everything possible to get back what it wanted: security of the presence of its mother. Second, it despaired by crying, withdrawing, becoming inactive, seeming to be in a deep state of mourning. If the separation still continued, the third phase was one of detachment. At first this could look like a recovery because the infant would begin to interact again with its surroundings. But, when the mother finally returned, the infant turned away listlessly, apparently having lost all interest in her. Or, if an infant or child has:

> **... the experience of becoming transiently**
> **attached to a series of nurses each of**
> **whom leaves ... he will in time act as if**
> **neither mother nor contact with humans has**
> **much significance for him. After a series of**
> **upsets at losing several mother figures to**
> **whom in turn he has given some trust and**
> **affection, he will gradually commit himself**

**less and less to succeeding figures and in
time will stop altogether attaching himself
to anyone. He will become increasingly
self-centered and, instead of directing his
desires and feelings towards people, will
become preoccupied with material things
such as sweets, toys, and food.**

John Bowlby, 1982, <u>Attachment</u>, p. 28

Perhaps those of us who have this fear of loss of the other, have also similarly experienced multiple unsuccessful (or, at least, not enduring) relationships and then, like the infants, become reluctant to continue to be open to this danger. Perhaps we also commit less and less each time, trusting less each time, until eventually we no longer attach or bond at all. Maybe we become more and more self-centered and preoccupied with material things. A succession of lost parent figures or a succession of unsuccessful romantic relationships might produce the same result.

FEAR OF LOSING THE SELF

**One woman was afraid to get more involved even though
the man that she was now dating was an interesting and a
sensitive man that had been introduced to her by a close
friend. She had been in a previous relationship that still
left her feeling wary. He was an older man who made her
feel secure, at least at the beginning. She liked feeling
needed, so she constantly waited on him, and everyone,
apologizing often for things not being good enough. The
harder she tried to please him, the more he expected of
her and the more he criticized whatever she was doing.
She really did want to be important to him, but to wait on
him hand and foot? Her family thought she had become
unrecognizable. She seemed to have changed from being
a bright and capable woman with a lot of friends, to now**

being fearful and isolating herself. One night he became angry and pushed her down to the floor so that she hurt her neck. She was completely stunned. But, after just a few moments, she got up, walked out the door, and never saw him again. His verbal abuse had not pushed her over the edge, but physical abuse sent a clear message. She wanted to have a relationship but she also saw that she'd lost her own self. Now, she wanted to learn to try again.

For some of us, then, amoraphobia is the fear of <u>losing ourselves</u> in relationships. Our fear is about loss of identity, loss of control, feeling engulfed, feeling dependent, feeling overly vulnerable. When we experience the closeness in the feelings associated with intimacy, rather than finding it gratifying, we find it frightening. It elicits the fear of being swallowed up, completely losing our identity. For example, a man is attracted from a distance to a woman who seems independent and self-sufficient, but when he gets up close, he becomes afraid of her strength and of being controlled. Or, the opposite, he becomes afraid when he sees that she also has vulnerabilities and needs, afraid he might have to spend too much of his time and energy on her and that he will end up engulfed or consumed by her. Similarly, a woman can be attracted to a man who is very romantic and emotional, but then, later on, feel overwhelmed by the intimacy and become afraid that he might end up being too needy and she won't be able to lead the independent life that she wants.

Some of us know that we have a tendency to become dependent in relationships and perhaps "choose" to be alone, or sabotage relationships, as a way of avoiding this. Maybe we lack a firm sense of our own individuality, or our identity, and fear becoming submerged into the identity of a partner. For others, the fear is that we'll be controlled, or that we'll have to struggle endlessly for power in the partnership, or we may fear the pressure to make a decision that will then turn out to be the wrong choice. Sometimes this is just because of a lack of skills for negotiating differences, leaving us thinking that we'll end up having to rely on, or be subjected to, coercive or bullying tactics — nagging, threatening, or guilt induction. These dysfunctional tactics just perpetuate our fear and our avoidance of intimacy.

Having to reveal personal things about ourselves or to compete for power – things that are essential in relationships – makes some of us feel extremely vulnerable. Studies show that a man with a high need to have power has more relationship break-ups than a man who is low in this need. This man is likely to be dissatisfied with partners and to anticipate problems before they even happen. He gets involved in serious relationships but they don't last and he is less likely to get married than men who are low in the need for power. These same tendencies didn't seem to be true with power-oriented women. Women might seek power differently and see having a relationship as part of their power rather than as competitive with it. This might also be true for men who seek power in politics or in other high visibility occupations since these are public, and thus vulnerable, arenas, where needing a strong partner to buffer some of the pain of demands and criticism can probably overcome the fear of having to share the power!

FEAR OF LOSING FREEDOM (AND LIMITING OPTIONS)

A couple had been dating for a number of years but the woman was reluctant to get married. She'd been married once before and her husband had passed away. She had lived a wonderful life as his wife but she'd since learned to enjoy her freedom. She loved her home, liked having things exactly the way she wanted them, loved not having to cook if she didn't feel like it, liked having people over when she wanted company or sitting and reading by herself when she didn't. Finally, she agreed to let her new mate move into the house with her. But, when moving day came, she was completely unable to help him in any way. She spent the entire day in a small room that she called her "library," rearranging the books on each shelf, positioning them alphabetically by author, then by title, and then creating an index file. She was terrified! Fortunately, both she and her new partner recognized this as useful obsessive-compulsive behavior for dealing with anxiety! Then

she even fell asleep next to her books on the couch.... The next morning they laughed and laughed about it together over breakfast, and they continued to laugh about it many more times in the years that followed.

Successful relationships require the ability to achieve a delicate balance between maintaining a sense of autonomy and privacy while still having the security of closeness and commitment. For some, this balance seems very difficult to achieve. We fear <u>entrapment</u>, that our options will become limited, or that we'll lose our freedom to live as we choose. This fear of losing our freedom sometimes only shows up at the point where the balance is in danger — maybe not until the moment that requires commitment. Then there can be a struggle, overt or covert, about whether or not to continue the relationship. Often this shows up in a paradoxical way, when one partner unexpectedly either moves toward getting closer or separating. For example, at significant turning points in life like the purchase of a home or the completion of one partner's education, sometimes a break-up is precipitated rather than things moving forward as expected. On the other hand, sometimes a partner being unfaithful can paradoxically provoke a decision to get married or an agreement to retake vows with renewed commitment.

Usually, as we continue to invest more in a relationship, we feel more commitment. And sometimes if we feel dissatisfied but continue to invest in the relationship anyway, we find that our feelings become more positive just as a result of our further investment. But if we fear losing our freedom, we can instead feel trapped by the situation, afraid that we're not really choosing to continue to invest but we're not seeing any other way out. Sometimes this conflict just comes from our inability to let go of our doubts, or from holding onto a notion that somewhere out there is a more gratifying partner (the Prince or the Princess). It can also be related to holding onto the wish that there really is a "free lunch" — we want to believe our choices don't have costs, our actions don't have consequences, our resources aren't limited, and that using our resources doesn't change them.

Every choice is a thousand relinquishments....
Unknown

Chapter Thirteen

Conflict and Sabotage

She: I want some time together.

He: I want some space.

She: We need to work on our relationship.

He: I work all week, I don't want to work weekends.

She: OK, but we need ground rules for weekends.

He: I hate ground rules. Why can't the rules just develop naturally?

She: They've already developed so naturally that I never see you.

He: But I need my freedom.

She: But I need some closeness.

He: You're already so close I feel like I can't breathe.

HAVING DIFFERENCES IN NEEDS and wishes is inevitable in relationships. But many of us complain that it's difficult to be understanding of each other's needs because we're so preoccupied with not wanting to feel that we're being pushed around or disrespected ourselves. When we don't have the skills to negotiate our differences, we resort to more coercive tactics: nagging, threatening, pouting, guilt. Unfortunately, these don't often change the objectionable behavior, but the use of the unpleasant tactic gets reinforced instead. Maybe we succumb to the tactic sometimes, changing our behavior temporarily, while at other times we rebel and won't change. This means we're giving an "intermittent positive response" to the tactic. We know from Behavior Modification that the best way to keep a behavior going (whether it's good or bad) is intermittent reinforcement. So, if we sometimes "reward" their coercive tactic and sometimes we don't, even when we think what we're doing is trying to cooperate at least some of the time, what we're really doing is "training" our partner to keep using that dreadful coercive technique to try to get us to change – over and over and over again.

Thus a destructive cycle is created. (a) An unwanted behavior occurs (we drank too much at an event and embarrassed our partner). (b) Instead of trying to negotiate, the offended person uses a coercive tactic to deal with it (our partner pouts and won't talk to us for three days). (c) The coercion is sometimes "rewarded" by the unwanted behavior stopping, if only for the moment (we hate the pouting and really want to ignore it as we often do, but instead we give our best remorseful apology, saying it was because we were so tired and didn't really want to go to the event in the first place). The pouting is actually the behavior that's getting intermittently rewarded and so it will most likely be used again. Meanwhile the unwanted behaviors that precipitated the problem have not been modified at all. We have not addressed either the drinking or how to handle feeling forced to go somewhere that we don't want to go. And we also haven't addressed using pouting as a coercive tactic. So, the same thing is very likely to happen again. The same conflict will continue over the same unresolved issues with no relief for either of us from the feeling of either being pushed around or disrespected.

A man greets his wife when she arrives home from work, and he sees that she is quite upset about something that happened. He sympathetically pours her a glass of wine, suggests that they postpone dealing with dinner until she feels better, and then goes into the den and turns on the television, wanting to give her some "space" to relax. But what she needs isn't space. She needs him to be there to listen. She feels alone and ignored. She

thinks he really isn't interested in her life. Weeks later, the man comes to the kitchen to get something to drink after work, feeling very annoyed about something that happened during the day. His wife decides to show him how to be caring. She follows him to the den, sits down next to him and begins asking him a lot of questions, trying to get him to tell her all about it. He wonders why she's invading his territory. He wants to turn on a ball game and forget about it until he is more relaxed. He feels smothered. Misunderstood. Without communicating with each other about this, their difference in styles is very hard to overcome. Each has to learn to give the partner what the partner wants and not what they would have wanted, even when it seems as if the situation is the same (Relationships Golden Rule).

Traditionally, women were said to deal with conflict by crying or by sulking or by criticizing men for their lack of understanding of feelings or for being insensitive to the effect that they have on others. Then men were traditionally seen as responding to this with anger, rejecting the woman's tears as manipulative, demanding a logical rather than an emotional response to a problem, and finding an unlimited myriad of excuses to delay any discussion of the matter. The women, further frustrated by this avoidant response, would insist on confronting the problem and the feelings <u>urgently</u>, which usually pushed the men even further in the opposite direction. Although traditional stereotypes might have changed, the same elements of conflict are still found even if the roles differ.

Studies show that when we're in a conflict-filled relationship, we're likely to blame our partner for problems and to deny any responsibility for our own poor behavior. If we're in a more satisfying relationship, we're more likely to overestimate our own part in the problem and try to correct it, as well as to negotiate about the other's objectionable behavior, therefore not falling into that negative non-productive cycle.

When her partner would say the "wrong thing" or would say something the "wrong way," rather than escalating it into a conflict, one woman would reply (with a twinkle

in her eye), "I think what you actually meant to say was..." and then give him the words that she wanted to hear him say. Her partner, very wisely understanding that he was being helped by her, and not controlled, would smile and begin again, "As I was saying,..." and he would repeat the words she had modeled for him. They both understood that, for the wise, relationships are a training program!

Besides differences in our wants, needs, and styles, what are the most common specific areas of conflict in relationships? With respect to personality conflicts, they all too often can be traced back to those very same personality characteristics that initially were so appealing in the beginning of the relationship, but later on become aggravating annoyances. With respect to other specific issues, the most commonly raised are almost always about money, sex, and children. But when it comes to sabotage, the underlying critical issues are usually about control (power struggles) and our dysfunctional beliefs.

Power Struggles

Relationships often flounder over the question of who tells who what to do when.

Jay Haley, 1963, <u>Strategies of Psychotherapy</u>

Struggles for power emerge in relationships when one partner is afraid of being controlled by the other. This usually happens if mutual trust hasn't yet fully developed, if a balance of power hasn't yet been achieved, or if circumstances cause the balance or established trust to change so much that the relationship is no longer in equilibrium.

Those of us who think of ourselves as powerful, traditionally men, are more likely to use direct power strategies in interactions, even in intimate relationships. Those who see ourselves as lacking power, traditionally women, are more likely to resort to indirect strategies, maybe feeling that's our only way to get what we want from a disadvantaged position. Women were traditionally taught: make a man think that our ideas are actually his; don't appear to know more than he does; let him feel dominant so he will feel needed and adequate as a leader. Recent research has shown that whether our views regarding power are traditional or not, this isn't as relevant to relationship satisfaction as whether we share similar views with our partner.

Studies also found that when one of us feels less involved in the relationship, we usually hold more power because we're less vulnerable. When we see options available outside the relationship, we're less dependent on the partner, so we have more power. Even when we strive for having equal power, or each having power in different areas, we still tend to lean toward one or the other dominating. And the more educated a woman is, the less likely it is that she thinks men have, or should have, more power than she has.

Although the "battle between the sexes" still permeates our culture, it's generally expressed with a sense of humor. If we take it too seriously, our struggle for power and our struggle for love can block one another. When we use power to manipulate life, we can block the possibility of being open to love. On the other hand, if we indiscriminately surrender to love, we can block our ability to have any power. For relationships to last, we need a balance of both, love and power. The battle is usually best resolved when we are both able to feel that we have some of the power in the relationship and that there is enough flexibility so that we can each be in control when it's necessary and appropriate.

One woman felt that she had taken too much power when it came to small daily decisions for her husband. She was glad that he left some things up to her but she was tired of always telling him such things as what to wear and what to eat. She agreed to try out getting <u>him</u> to decide what he wanted for lunch that day. So she went home and asked him what he felt like having to eat. He replied in his usual "whatever you want is fine" fashion. But she said she really wanted him to choose. He said, "You know I always like anything you make me,

dear." She persisted and said that she wanted him to make the decision. After a couple more rounds of this, he finally said, "Well, okay, I guess I'd like a turkey sandwich." So, she went into the kitchen and opened the refrigerator to take out the turkey. However, while she was there, she saw the fish that was left over from dinner and decided that they better eat that first! No one ever said that changing was easy!

Sabotage: Dysfunctional Beliefs

We have met the enemy and he is US!

(Pogo comic strip, 1970)

Many conscious as well as unconscious relationship beliefs, feelings, or behaviors (those that we learned in childhood as well as those that we learned from unsuccessful previous relationships) become the mindset that can sabotage our relationships. Many psychotherapy methods include the idea that we are influenced by the "messages" that we received from our parents or others during childhood. In Transactional Analysis, we identify "tapes" that we keep repeating as "scripts" over and over again. In Hypnosis, we use age regression to explore the layers covering up our vulnerable "child within." In Learning Theory, we investigate conditioned behaviors that we've developed since our "tabula rasa" (blank slate) of childhood. Control Mastery is based on the idea that we get negative messages when we're growing up, most of them well-intended, but many of them that are simply unconsciously passed on, probably from previous generations, and then these become unconscious beliefs that are harmful to us later in life. For example, if we're excessively punished and criticized as a child, we may then later convert this into a negative self-image. Even if we try to rebel against these negative messages, we often end up acting out what our parents "predicted," in spite of all of our efforts to resist.

Many messages from childhood get incorporated into our dysfunctional beliefs, feelings, and behaviors that can then sabotage our later relationships.

Some of these are listed below, with some blank spaces if you want to add your own.

ABOUT OURSELF

- Believing we don't really deserve to be with anyone.
- Believing we don't deserve to be happy because of some real or imagined guilt.
- Believing that to know us would not be to love us.
- Believing that anyone interested in us must not be worthwhile.
- Feeling afraid of being alone.
- Feeling afraid of failing.
- Feeling afraid of succeeding.
- Feeling continually discouraged and hopeless.
- Feeling depressed (and showing it) even while attending happy events.
- Being persistently unaware of our own behavior and patterns in relationships.
- Being so preoccupied with finding someone that we're trying too hard.
- Being overly passive for fear of being rejected.
- Being unapproachable (in looks or in actions).
- Being overdressed or acting more formal than is appropriate for the situation.
- Being underdressed or acting more casual than is appropriate for the situation.
- Being treated badly — and allowing it to continue to happen.
- Being the one who abandons a relationship out of fear that it might happen to us.
- Being self-blaming for not having found someone or for losing someone.
- Being self-punishing for having a successful career (believing it's not okay or not possible to have success in both career and relationship).
- Being self-defeating by not even trying or by giving up too easily.
- _____
- _____
- _____
- _____

ABOUT THE OPPOSITE SEX

- Believing in stereotyped ideas that keep us from seeing who someone really is.
- Believing that we can change the other person rather than changing ourself.
- Believing that the opposite sex should be approached with distrust.
- Believing that we should look for a partner who is "better" than us.
- Believing that no one is better than us.
- Believing that no one is good enough for us.
- Believing that we will only meet "losers."
- Believing that the Prince or Princess is coming and we just need to wait.
- Believing in some idea about who is our "type."
- Believing that there is only one right person for us.
- Believing that younger men or older women are not acceptable.
- Believing that how someone looks is everything.
- Believing that looks don't matter at all.
- Believing that someone with different views than us should be avoided.
- Feeling resentment or anger toward the opposite sex based on past situations or observations that aren't relevant in the current situation.
- Feeling disappointed by the opposite sex (and holding onto it).
- Feeling that the opposite sex is always to blame.
- Feeling that the opposite sex is never to blame.
- Feeling that our expectations should be met no matter how unrealistic or how idealistic they may be.
- Behaving in a stereotypical way with someone when that's not really who we are.
- _____
- _____
- _____
- _____

ABOUT LOVE AND RELATIONSHIPS

- Believing lovers can sense each other's needs without being told what they are.
- Believing that love will solve everything.
- Believing that love is always romantic.
- Believing that lust is really love.
- Believing that love is really lust.
- Believing that people always "just know" immediately whether or not it's right.
- Believing that relationships have a timetable and things should happen in a certain time frame.
- Feeling fearful of some undefined danger about love.
- Feeling confused about a relationship — and not trying to find out why.
- _____
- _____
- _____
- _____

ABOUT SEX

- Believing that true lovers have a perfect sexual connection.
- Believing that sex is only a biological drive.
- Believing that sex is just a type of recreation.
- Believing that sex is the only thing that's important.
- Believing that sex is not really very important.
- Believing that there's only one right method of sexual expression.
- Feeling afraid to say "no."
- Feeling afraid to say "yes."
- Feeling pressured to get involved sexually even when we are not really ready.
- Being sexual as a way of rewarding our partner.
- Being withholding of sex as a way of punishing our partner.
- Being sexual to meet other needs that may be real but aren't sexual.
- Being sexual to get romance or affection.

- Being sexual to get affirmation of our performance or prowess.
- Being inappropriately sexual because of inappropriate boundaries or values.
- Being non-sexual because of inappropriate boundaries or values.

- _____
- _____
- _____
- _____

ABOUT CONFLICT

- Believing that people don't change so it's useless to try to resolve differences.
- Believing that disagreements represent a lack of love.
- Believing that everything needs to be dealt with, analyzed, and interpreted.
- Believing that nothing needs to be dealt with, analyzed, or interpreted.
- Believing that we are right and the other person is wrong.
- Believing that compromise is only about settling or surrendering.
- Believing that we should never have to settle or surrender.
- Being argumentative as our standard reaction to everything.
- Being afraid of ever arguing or disagreeing about anything.
- Being violent or threatening, verbally or physically.

- _____
- _____
- _____
- _____

ABOUT RESPONSIBILITY

- Believing that we will have to give up all of our freedom.
- Believing that we won't have to give up any of our freedom.
- Believing that we have to stay in a relationship even if things end up going badly.
- Believing that we should leave a relationship as soon as things start going badly.

- Believing that giving is conditional — that what we give should be received or used in a certain way or it should be withdrawn.
- Believing that the work is in finding, not in maintaining, a relationship.
- Believing that a relationship grows without nourishing and caring for it.
- Believing that we don't need to acknowledge the other person's contributions.
- Believing that we don't have to communicate verbally.
- Believing that we don't have to listen.
- Believing that non-verbal communication doesn't count.
- Feeling overly fearful about having to be responsible for the other person.
- Feeling overly fearful about the dangers related to sex or pregnancy.
- Feeling overly cavalier about the dangers related to sex or pregnancy.
- Feeling overly fearful about sacrificing our freedom for the unknown.
- Being focused on what we get rather than on what we can give.
- Being too busy to find enough time for our partner or for the relationship.
- Being habitually unsatisfied.
- Being an observer of life rather than a participant.

- _____
- _____
- _____
- _____

ABOUT THE WORLD AROUND US

- Believing that we are somehow very different from everyone else.
- Believing that we can give up our friends because our partner will now meet all of our needs.
- Believing that we should follow our parents' expectations of us.
- Believing that we should seek the opposite of what our parents think is best.
- Believing that we should not do better than our parents did, especially the one of the same sex.
- Feeling proud of a relationship as a way of letting others know that we are

better than they are.

- Being unresolved in our relationship with our parent of the opposite sex.
- Being unresolved in our relationship with our parent of the same sex.
- Being involved with unavailable or married people while "waiting" for the right one to come along.
- Being involved with unavailable or married people, expecting them to change.
- Being a homebody or "couch potato" and not making any effort to meet people or go places.
- _____
- _____
- _____
- _____

CHAPTER FOURTEEN

To End or Not to End

**In the West, the media message via television
and movies often gives the impression that
quick, often impossibly romantic solutions to
real problems are possible. This may
predispose us as a culture to disillusionment
and disappointment when we are confronted
with the inevitable shortcomings of a real life
relationship. The emphasis in the more "new
age" elements of the culture seems to be more
on "moving on" when a relationship becomes
uncomfortable, rather than on working it out.**

**S. Boorstein, 1979, "Troubled Relationships,"
Journal of Transpersonal Psychology, 11, p. 135**

STRANGERS MEET – A FLIRTING look is noted – a date is requested
– dating begins – disclosure is tested – romance blooms – intimacy is explored –
trust develops – harmony is established – future plans are made – commitments
discussed – permanence tested – and then follows a proposal of marriage and
the promise of a life together.

More often than not, of course, this expected sequence of phases doesn't follow this nice path. Instead the relationship ends because we aren't able to accomplish this developmental path. Maybe we aren't able to achieve a real sense of feeling intimate or attached. Or maybe we <u>are</u> able to develop the intimacy and attachment but then we're unable, or unwilling for countless reasons, to sustain it over a period of time. Whether there's been a sexual relationship established, and even whether there's been a trial of living together, doesn't predict if the relationship will continue successfully. Nor does our report of being happy or satisfied at any given time predict if the partnership will be stable over time. All of these are only momentary assessments.

Research has found, however, that the most reliable predictors of the likelihood of a relationship continuing are: (a) that both partners are equally involved and equally invested in the relationship, (b) that the level of reward from the partnership is roughly equal for both, and (c) that the expected chance of marriage, or long-term commitment, is highly likely from the perspective of both partners. It was also found that we feel less uncertainty, and are therefore much less likely to break up, when we communicate often with one another, have at least some contact with our partner's family and friends, and when we see our partner as being generally similar to ourselves.

Of the many things that will keep relationships from progressing, two of the most important are holding onto anger or intolerance and being unable or unwilling to let go of our particular point of view. It seems that we get a choice: we either get to be "right" – or we get to be in a relationship.

Another view that tends to undermine relationships is the notion that there might be a more satisfying partner out there somewhere. Holding on to this thinking, whether consciously or unconsciously, not only interferes with our committing to the relationship but it also justifies continuing to look around. This is acceptable, maybe necessary, for reassurance in the early part of any relationship. But, later on, it can all too often result in provoking our partner's mistrust about our feelings for them, or even in us projecting our own doubts into some kind of imagined infidelity of our partner.

And then there is the issue of restlessness or boredom. When we are not paying enough attention to what's missing in our own life, and therefore we're not seeking what we need to be doing for ourselves, we can instead hold onto the belief that we would be so much happier if only our partner was more something or other, or if only our partner would do more (or less) of this or that, or if only some other thing....

It is said that love and hate are actually closely connected and that the opposite of love is really indifference. Sometimes when we convince ourselves that there must be someone else out there who would be better for us, or when we are unsatisfied with our own life as it is, we begin distancing from our partner rather than trying to resolve these issues, and our partner experiences it as indifference.

> **One man tried sharing his home with a woman that he had found appealing and fascinating while they were dating, but when she was living in his "castle," everything she did seemed to bother him. For months she was receptive and understanding and tried to gently encourage him to talk about what was bothering him. But he avoided her. He would busy himself with other things that needed taking care of. She tried cooking things that he liked, inviting friends over to join them, planning trips to their favorite places, getting tickets to shows or events. When he came home from work, she would greet him happily at the door with a smile and kiss. But, after a while, he wouldn't even look at her when she greeted him. He quickly kissed her on the cheek and brushed right past her, as if he wished she wasn't there. And..., pretty soon..., she wasn't.**

Women are more likely than men are to emphasize interpersonal problems as the reason a relationship ends, but both men and women attribute endings to differences in interests, differences in intelligence, differing ideas about marriage, wanting to be more independent, or wanting to be with someone else. The only issue that men are likely to raise more than women as the reason for ending a relationship is geographical distance.

Some of us do say that we actively deal with relationship dissatisfaction by trying to negotiate with our partner in an effort to improve things. But most of us are likely to describe dealing with dissatisfaction by passively waiting for improvement to happen, by passively letting things just deteriorate, by actively abusing the relationship, or by simply ending it, sometimes without any explanation. Why do we (especially men) say, "I'll call you," and then disappear? Most of us claim it's because we don't want to hurt the other person's feelings. But many of us, both men and women, admit that we really don't want to have to deal with the ending or that we just don't know how to go about it.

Research has also shown that endings are likely to occur at certain specific times of the year: May and June (the beginning of summer), September (the end of summer), and December and January (the beginning and end of the holidays). Most of the time, both partners will claim that it was _not_ a mutual break-up and that _we_ were the initiator. While it's usually the less involved person who actually initiates the ending, sometimes it's the more involved one who just becomes frustrated and eventually gives up. Usually, the feelings of the woman are a better predictor of what's going to happen than the feelings of the man, possibly because she's by nature a better barometer than he is, but mostly because her feelings will usually have a stronger effect on the relationship. A woman is more likely to initiate the ending regardless of whether she is the one who is less involved or more involved, while a man is unlikely to end it unless he's the one who is less involved. The initiator of a break-up is usually the one who ends up feeling freer, less depressed, and less lonely, but also is more likely to feel guilty. Remaining friends after a break-up is more likely to happen if the man is the one who ended it or if it was truly mutual. Men don't usually want to "be friends" when they are the one who is being left.

Studies also found that women don't generally fall in love as easily as men do but do tend to fall out of love more easily than men do. If a relationship isn't progressing, a woman is more likely to want to leave. Maybe this is because, traditionally, women were more dependent on marriage and were more limited in marriage-able years.

Women are more likely than men to grieve and despair and take more time before even considering getting involved again. Women are less likely to hold onto hoping that a rejecter "really still loves them." Overall, though, men tend to be the ones who are hit harder by a break-up. Even though we might see them going out again the day after a relationship has ended, they are three times more likely than women to commit suicide following a broken love affair. Maybe this is because, traditionally, men have tended to feel the need to seek an immediate substitute, and then, being less discriminating about their attractions, this sometimes leads to a poor choice, resulting in lowered self-esteem and even in despair.

So I want you to know some things about leaving people. It is fine to do so. Not wrong. And there are consequences. The consequences are that you take your "stuff" to the next relationship you have and recreate your experience. You then have another opportunity to become responsible for your experience of people. At that point you can come into responsibility or you can leave again. If you leave, the cycle repeats and you get another opportunity. Sooner or later you will realize, maybe, only if you do, that the source of your unpleasant experience of people is you.

Ron Smotherman, 1980,
<u>Winning Through Enlightenment</u>, p. 129-130

CHAPTER FIFTEEN

So What's Good About It?

When I was one-and-twenty
I heard a wise man say,
"Give crowns and pounds and guineas
But not your heart away;
Give pearls away and rubies
But keep your fancy free."
But I was one-and-twenty,
No use to talk to me.

When I was one-and-twenty
I heard him say again,
"The heart out of the bosom
Was never given in vain;
'Tis paid with sighs a plenty
And sold for endless rue."
And I am two-and-twenty,
And oh, 'tis true, 'tis true.

A. E. Housman, 1896

So WHY DO WE still persist in pursuing this love commitment – this entanglement – fraught with so many conflicts and obstructions and problems? Why is it not enough, as some propose, to just stay in the "falling in love" phase of a relationship and when that ends, look for someone else to fall in love with?

Well, it seems that if we can manage to get past all of the pitfalls and hazards, the positive side of a long-term committed relationship is still thought well worth the trouble. Most believe that it offers the promise of irresistible, enviable rewards. Theorists offer us the following ideas to describe what a "healthy" loving relationship can look like and the benefits we can experience if we manage to establish and sustain it. Just as is true for individuals who are continually developing, this is never a completed product, but a process that is always improving, growing, and changing. Partnership "actualization."

Being Friends

Having a strong foundation of the basics: doing things together, being accepting of one another, being dependable, understanding, supportive, comfortable to talk with. Men tend to emphasize the sharing of activities and interests, while women generally find emotional support to be the key ingredient. As close friends, we don't see one another as competitive (except in fun), we see mostly positive behaviors and traits in each other, and we usually overestimate how similar we are in our attitudes and beliefs.

Trusting

Evolving out of our past experiences with others as well as our interactions with our current partner, this essential ingredient develops as our relationship matures. It is the result of finding our partner to be reliable, dependable, and genuinely concerned with <u>mutually</u> providing the rewards that we both want from the relationship. It requires our willingness to take risks: to talk openly and candidly, to rely on the promises of our partner, and often to sacrifice some rewards in the present for the hope of gains in the future. With trust, we can also be around other people comfortably because our mutual respect allows for the open expression and handling of any jealousy or insecurity.

An important piece in developing this kind of trust is being motivated to act both cooperatively (that is, in the interests of the relationship, not just our own interests) and honestly (that is, being sincere and believable when we talk about our feelings as well as our future intentions). This allows us to feel comfortable enough to be vulnerable in the relationship when necessary. This becomes even more important when one partner has fewer resources than the other and so has to depend on cooperatively using the other's greater resources. Maybe because women have traditionally had this dependent role, we're likely to have a more integrated view of trust based on a combination of character (dependability), consistency of behavior (predictability), and feelings (faith), while men tend to be more romantic and less practical in their trust.

Although trust is a slow and often difficult foundation to build, it is notoriously very easy to destroy. And, once betrayed, it is even more difficult to re-build. Broken agreements and unmet expectations damage our trust, but what actually determines the ultimate health of a relationship is resilience. Trying to understand why an agreement was not kept or an expectation was not fulfilled, and then determining what to do about it. Together. This is what leads to an even stronger, often more realistic, relationship.

Having Faith

This isn't about religion but about having an underlying feeling of confidence and security in the strength and durability of the relationship. It includes an ability to believe in each other, knowing that we'll continue to act in loving and caring ways no matter what happens. Having this kind of faith has been shown to correlate with enduring happiness more than even qualities like being dependable and reliable.

Sharing Life

This starts with thinking as a pair ("we" or "us" rather than "I" or "me"), with the sense of continuity in the relationship that allows for anticipating the future and being able to make plans together. It means we are able to re-negotiate our expectations and agreements from time to time and also to understand that what benefits both of us as a couple also benefits each of us individually. There is a well-balanced flow of giving and sharing rather than it seeming one-sided or that either of us has a sense of giving things up for the other. We feel joy in spending time alone together, we have a desire to please one another, and we experience happiness from such things as mutually exploring new activities and interests.

Respecting Boundaries

Respecting the need for privacy, we're able to allow our partner to be alone some of the time. We each appreciate the other's ongoing development and are interested in – without being intrusive into – the other's activities. We both feel comfortable with our own identities as adults, and we can value and care about both our children and parents without permitting either one to interfere with our commitment as a couple. We explore our sexuality only within our partnership and as an expression of tenderness, affection, and love, as well as passion, sensuality, and playfulness. We do not use sex as a way of smoothing over unresolved conflicts or as a weapon to get compliance.

Expressing Feelings

As partners, we experience and share a wide range of feelings together, from joy and laughter to tears and sadness. We aren't intimidated by the expression of emotion. We can comfort and soothe each other as well as confront and express our anger to one another. We share optimism, enjoy good-natured teasing, and occasionally see a sense of the absurdity and unreasonableness of life. We cooperatively find ways to cope with painful and even devastating emotional situations, supporting our own and our partner's strengths, and reaching out to resources outside of our relationship when we need to.

Communicating Ideas

This is about clearly expressing our wishes and expectations, without demanding or being controlling, and with each of us being responsible for our own statements, not expecting our partner to be a mind-reader. Our communication is genuine. We ask each other for feedback and for clarification, and we talk through our conflicts and decisions that need to be made. We are able to allow for our differences of opinion without being disparaging or thinking that our partner's ideas are somehow unworthy.

Negotiating

We discuss whatever issues arise, listen to one another's viewpoint, and then we negotiate. That is, we try to resolve problems at the highest possible level, getting as much input as possible from us both, so that we feel that we're getting most of what we want (probably not all), instead of feeling that a "compromise" means we're giving in.

Sharing Power

Feeling equally matched, we tend to shift back and forth in taking the lead, with equality and happiness being more important than being "right." We value our ability to reason and persuade, while discouraging manipulation, downgrading, and coercion, as well as acquiescing. And, although there's a clear sense of firm attachment between us, we both know that we can still have a meaningful life without the other, when necessary, without living vicariously either through our partner or through our children.

Enjoying Humor

Among the most important factors in a satisfying relationship is having a capacity for playfulness. Pet names, shared private jokes, playful insults, make-believe fighting, and other forms of play provide a balance between having too much intimacy and having too much distance. We're cautious, though, about the pitfalls involved in using humor in a relationship. We don't use it as a way of avoiding issues, hurting, or embarrassing one another, or if the timing or the circumstances are inappropriate. Although we probably each contribute differently to the humor, we're able to keep it from getting unbalanced with one of us always in the same role rather than it changing back and forth.

Believing in Something Bigger Than Ourselves

One final and very significant ingredient is the sharing of some clear set of beliefs about life. This isn't necessarily spiritual, but it is some sense of relatedness to the past and to the future. It's a feeling of belonging to some universal concept of humanity. We are aware of our own mortality, the inevitability of death, and we want both together and individually to fully experience meaning and purpose in our lives. Together we travel and explore the challenging path of life, helping one another to maintain an overall sense of tranquility, a sense of inner peace. Together we engage in projects bigger than just our relationship, from building a home, to having children, to participating in the community or in the world.

CHAPTER SIXTEEN

So What's Wrong
With Being Single?

NOTHING! THERE ARE MANY of us who are leading wonderful lives as singles and are perfectly content with remaining that way: the "happily un-married." Many who are cherishing independence as well as enjoying the company of friends, family, and lovers. Some who have a partner but still prefer living alone. Some who feel our life goals might not be accomplished if we were committed to being in a marriage. Some who just enjoy being on our own, doing whatever we want whenever we want.

There are many of us who have previously been married and are very happy to be single again, having another chance at deciding just how we want to live our life and with whom. Considering trying marriage again is not out of the question, but for now we're in no hurry to get there.

"The Second Time Around"

Then there are many others who are finding that a second (or even a third) try at marriage seems to work much better than the first one did. We've learned so much more about ourselves and about what we have to give to someone else as well as what we can realistically expect from a partner and a commitment. We now understand so much more about what we're getting into and about how to manage it wisely – sometimes even with much more complicated circumstances including an ex-spouse, stepchildren, extended families, demanding jobs, having to combine homes, and so on. Perhaps we were lucky and found someone special who is clearly more suitable than our first choice. Perhaps we discovered that we just don't really like being on our own, so we're now more willing to accept whatever problems we might have to face with someone new. Maybe we found out we're more dependent than we thought on having companionship or the helpfulness of a partnership. Or maybe we just simply fell in love again and we couldn't resist – we didn't want to resist – committing to our new love.

So What About The Rest Of Us?

So, there are some of us who really don't want to be married, and there are some of us who keep finding new partners even when one of them doesn't work out, so why is it that there are still some who are <u>unwillingly</u> remaining single? Some who say that we're interested in a partnership, but we still just can't seem to get to the finishing line. Or the starting line....

Are we less attractive? Less interesting? Less fun to be with? Are we less smart? Too smart? Too wimpy? Are we not sexy enough? Too sexy? Too immature? Are we too emotional? Too unemotional? Not kind enough? Are we too difficult? Too picky? Too rebellious?

My guess, in thinking about many of the single and married people that I've met, would be that there really are no differences. That none of these questions apply. It's just a circumstance of luck, just happening to meet the "right" person at the right time.

However, I decided to do a research study (some years ago) to find out if maybe some of this question could be answered, even just partially. I compared a group of men and women in midlife who had <u>never been married</u> with a group of their peers (similar background and in the same age range) that <u>were married</u>. What, if anything, would characterize those who remained unmarried in spite of proclaiming the desire to marry? Why did this apparently unwanted circumstance occur to some but not others?

Based on the issues that have been discussed in the previous chapters, I chose to address four possible factors.

Were the singles any more likely to have had problems related to early parenting or early family relationships? Were they any more likely to have experienced traumatic life events? Were they any more likely to be perfectionists or to have idealistic beliefs that might affect their expectations in relationships? Were they any more inclined to try to avoid intimacy or commitment because of having fears of loss including the fears of abandonment, engulfment, or loss of freedom? And, also, would there be any gender differences between the men and the women with respect to any of these issues?

The following summarizes the interesting conclusions that I found. If you would like to read about this in more depth, the details are provided in Appendix B.

Conclusions

From the data collected, it was possible to conclude that the midlife singles did, in fact, differ from their married peers on almost all of these dimensions! Although there weren't any differences in their early parenting or family relationships, they were more likely to report having heard both negative and idealistic "messages" about relationships during their childhood. They were more likely to have experienced a traumatic event or events that might have negatively influenced them in their future relationships. They were more likely to admit having beliefs about intimate relationships that were idealistic and/or perfectionistic. And they were more likely to report having fears that are related to loss.

Certainly there were some limitations to the study, but the data definitely did validate these ideas. We could see a picture of someone who idealistically searches for the perfect partner and yet fears abandonment, engulfment, or loss of freedom — all of which are necessary potential risks in establishing any intimate committed relationship. The research results were even strong enough to propose that they could, at least to some extent, be generalized to other singles populations, including those who were previously married but unsuccessful in further attempts to make that commitment again.

The importance of the underlying wish for the ideal — the perfect mate — seemed clear, but how it developed was not. The unresolved bonding and separating explanation was not supported by the results on their parenting relationships but other areas of the data did show that this still might have had some influence. Maybe the singles were more susceptible to unrealistic expectations learned from romantic movies or family shows on television because of all of the "messages" that they heard from their parents about themselves and about intimate relationships. Or maybe they would overreact to situations because they wanted to believe that the negative messages passed on by their families were not really true after all — and they wanted to prove it.

Of course it's hard to know whether such beliefs are learned from our upbringing or whether some of us are just more inclined toward idealistic or perfectionistic thinking. It's hard to know whether these lead us to have unrealistic expectations or to frustrate our ability to establish connections in the complicated world of relationships. Maybe these same traits might make some of us more suitable for successes or accomplishments that would be more difficult for our peers that are more "tied down" in their marriages.

Also, Equity Theory tells us that we have to feel that we have enough to offer in the "marketplace" to make a fair exchange for the partnership we're seeking. Maybe some feel that we don't have sufficient assets to be worthy of our "perfect" mate, even if that's what we continue to want. And, when we're so critical of ourselves, maybe we're also less capable of accepting the flaws of another long enough to be able to just relax and enjoy the better parts of a satisfying and fulfilling relationship. Since these traits and fears are often unconscious, this can account for those who express interest in marrying but don't seem to achieve it.

It can also be speculated that people who do marry and remain married might have some traits and fears of a completely different variety — like the fear of being alone, of emptiness or isolation. Perhaps we commit to a partnership (or even to serial partnerships) to assure ourselves of having someone to depend on, to assure ourselves of having companionship and security, out of our own fears of facing life on our own.

And so there remains the idiosyncratic question:

Is the grass really greener?

Everyone is different. If <u>your</u> answer is yes, that the other side of the fence still looks like where you would like to be, I hope that you have found some of the "tips" in this book helpful to you in your relationships ahead — and I wish for you that a loving and wonderful mate is about to emerge!

APPENDIX A

The Questionnaire

MIDLIFE RELATIONSHIPS QUESTIONNAIRE

DIRECTIONS: Please provide the following information by filling in the blanks or circling the number of the most accurate category, writing in information wherever necessary to clarify your response.

Age _____ Sex _____ Residence _____

Ethnic origin   1. Caucasian

                2. Black

                3. Hispanic

                4. Asian

                5. American Indian

                6. Other _____

Religion   1. Protestant

          2. Catholic

          3. Jewish

          4. Other _____

          5. None

Education   1. High school

           2. Trade / vocational

           3. College

               Number of years _____ Degree _____

           4. Graduate school

               Number of years _____ Major _____

                                             Degree _____

           5. Postgraduate school

               Number of years _____ Major _____

                                             Degree _____

Occupation _____

Income
1. Under $20,000
2. $20,001 to 30,000
3. $30,001 to 40,000
4. $40,001 to 50,000
5. $50,001 to 75,000
6. $75,000 to 100,000
7. Over $100,000

Siblings
1. None
2. Brother(s) Age(s) _____
3. Sister(s)   Age(s) _____

Children
1. No
2. Yes   Age(s) _____

IF SINGLE:

Are you currently cohabiting?
1. No
2. Yes: Length of time _____

Have you previously cohabited?
1. No
2. Yes: Number of times _____
        Longest time _____

IF MARRIED:

How long have you been married? _____

Have you previously been married?
1. No
2. Yes: Number of times _____
        Longest time _____

DIRECTIONS: Please use the following adjectives to describe your family when you were growing up. (If your natural parents were not the ones who raised you, specify whom you are describing.) Rate by circling the number that most accurately fits.

Describe how your MOTHER was with you when you were growing up:

	DEFINITELY	MAINLY	MORE OFTEN	EQUAL	MORE OFTEN	MAINLY	DEFINITELY	
1. Accepting	1	2	3	4	5	6	7	Rejecting
2. Affectionate	1	2	3	4	5	6	7	Reserved
3. Realistic	1	2	3	4	5	6	7	Idealistic
4. Straightforward	1	2	3	4	5	6	7	Manipulative
5. Calm	1	2	3	4	5	6	7	Easily upset
6. Communicative	1	2	3	4	5	6	7	Withdrawn
7. Supportive	1	2	3	4	5	6	7	Critical
8. Trusting	1	2	3	4	5	6	7	Suspicious
9. Easily pleased	1	2	3	4	5	6	7	Perfectionistic
10. Respect for privacy	1	2	3	4	5	6	7	Intrusive
11. Cooperative	1	2	3	4	5	6	7	Controlling
12. Encouraging	1	2	3	4	5	6	7	Pessimistic

Describe how your FATHER was with you when you were growing up:

	DEFINITELY	MAINLY	MORE OFTEN	EQUAL	MORE OFTEN	MAINLY	DEFINITELY	
1. Accepting	1	2	3	4	5	6	7	Rejecting
2. Affectionate	1	2	3	4	5	6	7	Reserved
3. Realistic	1	2	3	4	5	6	7	Idealistic
4. Straightforward	1	2	3	4	5	6	7	Manipulative
5. Calm	1	2	3	4	5	6	7	Easily upset
6. Communicative	1	2	3	4	5	6	7	Withdrawn
7. Supportive	1	2	3	4	5	6	7	Critical
8. Trusting	1	2	3	4	5	6	7	Suspicious
9. Easily pleased	1	2	3	4	5	6	7	Perfectionistic
10. Respect for privacy	1	2	3	4	5	6	7	Intrusive
11. Cooperative	1	2	3	4	5	6	7	Controlling
12. Encouraging	1	2	3	4	5	6	7	Pessimistic

Rate your parents' relationship with <u>each other</u> when you were growing up:

1. Very happy	1	2	3	4	5	6	7	Very unhappy
2. Very stable	1	2	3	4	5	6	7	Very unstable
3. Very encouraging	1	2	3	4	5	6	7	Very discouraging

DIRECTIONS: Sometimes people get spoken or unspoken "messages" about relationships when they are growing up. Please circle the number of any of the following that were part of your upbringing.

1. Men only want women for sex.
2. Women only want men for money.
3. The opposite sex will leave you if you give them what they want.
4. The opposite sex will like you better if you treat them badly.
5. Men can't be trusted.
6. Women can't be trusted.
7. Men and women don't really understand each other.
8. Boys will be boys.
9. You are just like your mother.
10. You are just like your father.
11. You will hurt your mother if you say or do that.
12. You will hurt your father if you say or do that.
13. You will be a great catch.
14. You will make someone a wonderful husband/wife.
15. You will scare away the opposite sex if you are too _____.
16. No one will ever want you.
17. No one will ever put up with you.
18. No one is good enough for you.
19. Don't marry someone like I did.
20. Don't get tied down.
21. Don't get married just to have children.
22. Don't settle for second best.
23. Don't enjoy yourself too much.
24. Don't love anyone but me.
25. Don't do better than I did.
26. Marriage is nothing but trouble.

27. Work comes before family.

28. Someday your prince/princess will come.

29. Others (please specify:)

_____.

_____.

_____.

_____.

30. None of these apply.

DIRECTIONS: Circle the number of any of the following that you have experienced and give your approximate age at the time it occurred. (Optional — If you would be willing to clarify your response further, please use the space provided below.)

AGE

_____ 1. Death of a parent

_____ 2. Death of a brother/sister

_____ 3. Death of a relationship partner

_____ 4. Parents divorced

_____ 5. Parents separated

_____ 6. Parents argued frequently

_____ 7. Father had a drinking problem

_____ 8. Mother had a drinking problem

_____ 9. Serious illness/accident/injury of parent

_____10. Serious illness/accident/injury of brother/sister

_____ 11. Serious illness/accident/injury of partner

_____ 12. Serious illness/accident/injury (self)

_____ 13. Unplanned pregnancy (self or partner)

_____ 14. Abortion (self or partner)

_____ 15. Adoption

_____ 16. Severe depression

_____ 17. Suicide attempt

_____ 18. Very unhappy love affair

_____ 19. Broken engagement

_____20. Broken engagement at the last minute

_____ 21. Family violence

_____ 22. Child abuse

_____ 23. Incest/child sexual abuse

_____ 24. Sexual abuse as adult

_____ 25. Rape

_____ 26. Alcohol abuse

_____ 27. Drug abuse

_____ 28. Armed combat

_____ 29. Other (please specify:)

_____

_____

_____

Comments:

_____

_____

_____

DIRECTIONS: Describe yourself with respect to close relationships with the opposite sex by circling the number that most accurately fits.

1 = Definitely yes   2 = Mainly yes   3 = Mainly no   4 = Definitely no

1   2   3   4   Arguing or fighting makes me think the relationship is in trouble.

1   2   3   4   My partner wants more time away from me than I am comfortable with.

1   2   3   4   I worry about what will happen if the relationship doesn't work out.

1   2   3   4   I keep from getting too involved because there's always a chance it might end.

1   2   3   4   I tend to be "too nice" for fear that my partner might leave.

1   2   3   4   I tend to get taken advantage of because I don't want to lose my partner.

1   2   3   4   I seem to need a lot of reassurance that my partner wants to be with me.

1   2   3   4   I tend to accept being mistreated for fear that my partner will leave otherwise.

1   2   3   4   I am afraid of being abandoned.

1   2   3   4   I am afraid my partner will leave me because I won't be able to please him/her.

1   2   3   4   I am uncomfortable spending time "doing everything together" with my partner.

1   2   3   4   When my partner is very affectionate, I want to back away.

1   2   3   4   I feel the need for more private time away from my partner.

1   2   3   4   I feel smothered.

1   2   3   4   I don't like it when my partner wants to talk about everything.

1   2   3   4   I don't like to refer to my partner and myself as "we."

1   2   3   4   I am uncomfortable using affectionate names.

1   2   3   4   I tend to want to spend a lot of time with friends other than my partner.

1   2   3   4   I worry that my hobbies and pastimes will be forgotten because of my involvement with my partner.

1   2   3   4   I resent it when my work suffers because of my relationship.

1   2   3   4   I feel my partner is trying to control my life.

1   2   3   4   Depending on my partner makes me uneasy.

1   2   3   4   I worry about losing my independence.

1   2   3   4   I feel like running away.

1   2   3   4   I want to date outside the relationship.

1   2   3   4   I like to flirt with people other than my partner.

1   2   3   4   I seem to arrange my schedule to stay somewhat unavailable to my partner.

1   2   3   4   I resent feeling like I have to give things up for the relationship.

1 = Definitely yes   2 = Mainly yes   3 = Mainly no   4 = Definitely no

1 2 3 4   Making choices is painstaking for me.

1 2 3 4   I tend to want what I don't have.

1 2 3 4   I tend to not want what I do have.

1 2 3 4   I keep feeling that there may be someone else better for me.

1 2 3 4   I tend to feel tied down.

1 2 3 4   I tend to feel like I've lost my freedom.

1 2 3 4   I'm uncomfortable when my partner must make decisions that affect me.

1 2 3 4   I miss being single when I'm involved with someone.

1 2 3 4   I wonder if anyone would really be suitable for me.

1 2 3 4   When someone is really interested in me, I lose interest.

1 2 3 4   I tend to avoid doing things that have to be planned in advance.

1 2 3 4   Compromise feels like "settling" for something I don't really want.

1 2 3 4   When I make a decision, I tend to worry about options I didn't choose.

1 2 3 4   I tend to wish I could be in two places at once.

1 2 3 4   I believe in love at first sight.

1 2 3 4   Finding my "soul mate" has been important to me.

1 2 3 4   There aren't very many people that are my "type."

1 2 3 4   I believe there would only be a few right people for me.

1 2 3 4   Having the right "chemistry" has been important to me.

IF SINGLE, please complete the following (if married, see below).

DIRECTIONS: Please circle the number of any of the following that describe why you are unmarried and then check the five that seem to be the most important.

1. Hostility toward the opposite sex
2. Emotional involvement with parents
3. Always find something wrong with partners
4. Fear of being "tied down"
5. Unwilling to assume responsibility
6. Unable to find the right person
7. Don't want to lose privacy
8. Fear of being "smothered
9. Unable to sustain lasting relationship
10. Occupation prevents meeting people
11. Taking care of parent/sibling
12. Never had the opportunity
13. Don't want to repeat parents' marriage
14. Remaining open to new opportunities
15. Unhappy previous relationship
16. Don't want to chance divorce
17. Don't understand the opposite sex
18. Availability of birth control
19. Difficult to limit choices
20. Don't approve of institution of marriage
21. Don't want to risk getting hurt
22. Those I'm interested in aren't available/already taken
23. Those I'm interested in aren't interested in me
24. Not interested in those interested in me
25. Hostility toward marriage
26. Not ready
27. Interferes with career goals

28. Physical unattractiveness
29. Afraid of abandonment
30. Afraid of rejection
31. Social inadequacy
32. Want to maintain freedom
33. Financial problems
34. Poor health
35. Unrealistic expectations
36. Availability of sex
37. Death of fiance
38. Try too hard
39. Don't have time
40. Economic independence
41. Too idealistic/romantic
42. Unlucky
43. I'm doing something wrong
44. Something is wrong with me
45. Don't want children
46. Fear of intimacy
47. Fear of commitment
48. Like being alone
49. Fear of being dependent
50. Other

IF MARRIED, please list the reasons why you married:

_____

_____

_____

_____

_____

_____

EVERYONE: Is there anything that wasn't on this questionnaire that you would like to add?

_____

_____

_____

_____

_____

_____

_____

_____

_____

APPENDIX B-1

My Research: Summary

THE PURPOSE OF MY research was to address individuals in the early part of the midlife transition who had never been married, and then to compare them with their married counterparts in the same age range. What, if anything, would characterize these singles who have remained unmarried into midlife in spite of their own proclaimed desire to marry? Why would this apparently unwanted circumstance occur to some people but not to others? Are they any more likely than their married counterparts to have had any problematic early parenting relationships? Have their lives included more experiences of traumatic life events? Are they more likely to have idealistic and perfectionistic beliefs that might affect their expectations of others as well as themselves? Are they inclined to avoid intimacy or commitment because, compared to their married counterparts, they have more fears of loss related to abandonment, engulfment, or loss of freedom? And are there any gender differences with respect to any of these issues?

The study examined these issues as four factors that could possibly offer some further understanding about never-married singles during midlife. The intent was to establish the presence or absence of any of these differences without attempting to assess if there is any causality. That is, if subjects did differ significantly on any of the factors, it still couldn't be determined whether the factors influenced people to remain single or whether people who remain single tend to become characterized by these traits. Also, the results might not be applicable across socioeconomic or cultural strata since the subjects were generally well-educated, predominantly white, and middle class. The population was 35-45 year olds, considered to be in the "midlife decade," that time when a shift from youth to middle age is supposed to be accomplished. This age span was chosen since they had already passed what was considered the normative age for marrying, and, for women, the "biological clock" period that was acknowledged to be the safest time for bearing children.

The first two hypotheses were that singles would differ from married subjects in their views of their parents and their parents' relationship, and that these views would be more likely to be either highly positive or highly negative. These two ideas were not confirmed by the data. Singles did tend to have more negative views, but the difference was not statistically significant. However, all of the remaining hypotheses were validated by the results.

The third hypothesis, also related to early parenting, was about "messages" from childhood that characterized intimate relationships either in a negative or an idealistic way. This was found to be statistically different for the groups, with singles reporting having been told many more dysfunctional messages than married participants, and with females in both groups reporting more of these messages than males.

The fourth hypothesis proposed that singles would be more likely than marrieds to have experienced traumatic life events. This was also validated, with single subjects reporting significantly more of the listed trauma, and again with females reporting more of these events than males.

The results also supported all of the hypotheses that were related to personality characteristics. Both the female and the male singles were significantly more likely than their married counterparts to acknowledge having beliefs that were idealistic or perfectionistic as well as to select items representing all three types of fear of loss that were examined. There was only one variable among these that showed any significant differences based on gender and this was fear of abandonment, with single females being the most likely to report having this fear.

APPENDIX B-2

My Research:
Recruitment of Participants

LETTER TO PARTICIPANTS

Mid-life Relationships Questionnaire

Dear Participant,

As a doctoral student in clinical psychology at the California School for Professional Psychology in Berkeley, I am doing my dissertation research on relationships in mid-life. Participants in this study must be between 35 and 45 years old and must meet the following criteria:

<u>For Singles</u>

1. Never previously married (e.g., **<u>not</u>** divorced or widowed).

2. Predominantly heterosexual in orientation (during at least the past five years).

3. Experienced in at least one significant close relationship that lasted more than one year.

4. Not currently cohabiting for more than one year.

5. Interested in the possibility of marrying.

For Markeds

1. Currently married for at least two years.
2. Not separated.

Participation involves filling out the attached questionnaire that will take approximately one hour. **Please do not put your name on the questionnaire**. You may return it to the place where you received it or you may mail it to…. If you would like to receive a summary of the results of this research, please fill out the attached mailing label with your name and address. To assure the anonymity of your questionnaire, you may return the label separately.

Any questions you may have or any concerns that may arise as a result of your participation in this study may be addressed to me in care of the above address or you may contact me at….

Your involvement in this research will remain completely confidential and is in no way related to your membership or affiliation with any organization that is allowing the solicitation of participants. This is entirely voluntary; you may choose not to turn in your questionnaire or you may choose not to answer any question if it is particularly difficult for you to do so.

Your assistance with this research is greatly appreciated. Thank you very much for your time and interest.

Sincerely,

Marilyn Cohen

Licensed Clinical Social Worker

Ph.D. Candidate in Clinical Psychology

ANNOUNCEMENTS

The following announcements appeared in newsletters, on bulletin boards, and on radio news broadcasts.

Research: 35-45 year olds. If you have **never been married** (but are interested) or if you are currently married (for at least two years) and if you would be willing to participate in a doctoral dissertation research study by completing a questionnaire, please send your name and address to Mid-life Relationships, P. O. Box.... Thanks! Marilyn Cohen.

(Graduate school newspaper) **Dissertation Help Wanted** – If you are 35-45 years old and a) have never been married or b) are currently married for at least two years, I would appreciate your participation in my dissertation questionnaire on mid-life relationships. It explores why some people have remained single and others have married. It takes about 15 minutes and can be picked up and returned to my mailbox in the section for extension students. Thank you very much. Marilyn Cohen.

(Singles newsletter) In another academic endeavor, Marilyn Cohen, a graduate student at the California School of Professional Psychology, is compiling statistics for her doctoral dissertation on the subject of mid-life relationships. She is looking for subjects who are from 35 to 45 years of age, and who meet the following criteria: never married, experienced in at least one significant close relationship which lasted more than one year, not currently cohabiting for longer than a year, and interested in the possibility of marrying. If you meet these criteria, please contact Marilyn at ... or write to her at ... or call the office and we will relay the message to Marilyn. Participation involves filling out an anonymous questionnaire, which takes only a few minutes. Arrangements can be made for you to receive the results of the study. Your participation will be much appreciated by Marilyn, as you will readily understand from memories of your own graduate work.

(Radio station) Wanted: Men and women aged 35 to 45 who've never been married. Clinical worker Marilyn Cohen of ... is studying the so-called mid-life crisis as it relates to relationships: "I'm particularly interested in the never-married group because they really haven't been studied before. There have been a lot of studies on people who are in mid-life and having some kind of a crisis. Most of the studies presume that they are people who are married already." Questions Cohen would like to answer, for example — are middle-aged singles afraid of intimacy, happy to be alone, or maybe unlucky? The survey is anonymous and we'll have results for you. Again it's for singles aged 35 to 45. For a copy of the survey just stop by....

(Radio station) Doctoral candidate Marilyn Cohen believes studies on relationships and the so-called mid-life crisis have left out one key group, those aged 35 to 45 who've never married: "That's when you begin to see a lot of people who have been in some profession changing to another one, or who haven't been in a profession wanting to be, or people who've been mothers who now want to be career people, or, you know, all of those kind of changes." And so in completing her doctoral dissertation Cohen is asking ... listeners who fit that category to complete a short survey. For example: Yes or no, men only want women for sex or women can't be trusted. The survey is anonymous and you can pick one up here at.... We'll have the results for you later.

APPENDIX B-3

My Research: Variables and Hypotheses

ALTHOUGH MANY OF THE research studies that I reviewed provided some interesting information about relationships, and a few offered some understanding about midlife relationships, they never seemed to answer the question about why some people tend to remain unattached (or maybe stay married only briefly) while most of their counterparts did marry and stay married (or, if they were widowed or divorced, they married again). The research data didn't characterize whether the singles were in some way different, other than that they hadn't committed to and then maintained an enduring marriage.

So the investigation that interested me was to compare single men and women to married men and women of similar age and background, as well as to compare the singles to one another, to see if there were any similarities or differences in their life experience or in their own internal characteristics. Four specific issues were chosen and addressed. Two were environmental issues: (1) early family relationships and (2) traumatic life experiences. Two were personality traits: (3) idealism/perfectionism and (4) fear of loss. Of course, these don't include all of the possible explanations for this concern, nor were they completely independent from each other or from numerous other possible variables. But they were chosen based on earlier theories and research, as well as from writings in the popular press, as influences that could potentially be both applicable and interesting. The background for these influences has been described in the chapters of this book. The following briefly describes how it was set up in my study.

Environmental Influence – Early Family Relationships

The first environmental issue was about relationships within a person's family of origin and it examined some of the possible unconscious influences that this could have on mate selection. There wasn't any attempt to actually compare the characteristics of parents to the characteristics of spouses of the married subjects or to prior relationship partners of the singles (they weren't currently involved in a relationship if they were in the study). However, all participants were asked to describe their parents, including their physical appearance and temperament, the nature of the parent-child relationship as they saw it, and their perception of how their parents related to one another.

Since previous research showed that perceptions about marriage and pathology in marital relationships <u>are</u>, in fact, passed down from generation to generation, this study examined the conscious and unconscious "messages" that participants may have received during their childhood that might have influenced their adult relationships with the opposite sex or their feelings of self-esteem in social situations.

Also, theories about the process of "separation and individuation" from parents propose that mate selection might be based on a child's bonding experience with his or her parents and then later how they differentiate (separate themselves), especially from the parent of the opposite sex. These theories provided some of the underlying themes in this part of the research: the search for the "ideal" mate (trying to either replace the "ideal" parent or else trying to make up for the less than ideal one) and the confidence or the fear associated with intimacy and commitment. For example, my thinking was that if the single subjects had unresolved issues about bonding and separating, maybe they would describe their parents in more extremes, either more positively or more negatively, than the married subjects would.

So, the first environmental consideration was family influences during childhood, looking specifically at how subjects described each of their parents along a number of both physical and personality dimensions, how they described their own relationship with each parent, how they described their parents' relationship with one another, and what overt and covert messages they might have heard about intimate relationships and the opposite sex.

HYPOTHESIS #1:   Singles and marrieds are likely to differ in their views of their parents and/or their parents' relationship.
HYPOTHESIS #2:   Singles are more likely than marrieds to view their parents and/or their parents' relationship as either highly negative or highly positive.
HYPOTHESIS #3:   Singles are more likely than marrieds to report receiving messages in their childhood that might characterize intimate relationships in either a negative or an overly idealistic way.

Environmental Influence - Traumatic Life Experiences

The second environmental factor that I explored was the participants' exposure to traumatic experiences.   Most theorists agree that the after-effects of trauma include emotional numbing, withdrawal, and problems with intimacy. Although it's very difficult to correlate a particular traumatic experience with later issues, a traumatic event can be seen as one factor that increases someone's vulnerability to similar events in the future.   My study included a variety of traumatic experiences as well as common daily stresses of life to see if there were any differences between single and married subjects in their exposure to the events, and also to see whether singles would attribute their unmarried status to these events in any way.   Several traumatic events that seemed especially likely to impact personal relationships in adulthood were particularly examined: sexual abuse, parental violence and/or divorce, and experiences of loss.

Earlier research showed that victims of childhood sexual abuse or violence were vulnerable to getting involved in abusive relationships in adulthood and that deprivation of a relationship with one's parent can also result in later difficulty. Based on this, my research proposed that those raised in homes with troubled relationships might be more likely to keep seeking a relationship but then have trouble sustaining or staying satisfied with it. However, whether these individuals would actually be subjects who were single or whether they would more likely be found in troubled marriages couldn't be determined in this study since there weren't any measures of marital satisfaction. However, single subjects were asked if they thought their parents' marriage was a contributing factor to their own single status.

The study also examined whether losing a parent, among the many other types of trauma and loss, might be any more likely to have occurred in the lives of single subjects as compared with married subjects. Since traumatic losses that occur in adulthood have also been shown to correlate with people having difficulty in relationships, these losses were also included to see whether there were any significant differences between the two subject groups.

HYPOTHESIS #4: Singles are more likely than marrieds to have experienced and to report traumatic events that might negatively influence intimate relationships.

Personality Influence – Idealism/Perfectionism

Without also understanding the contribution of certain personality factors, it is hard to know if environmental factors can explain why some people marry while others don't. It's also hard to know if certain events might actually cause certain personality traits to develop – or if the events simply have more impact on people who are already constitutionally predisposed to reacting to them.

The next part of the study examined whether there were differences between the single and the married subjects on the personality factors of idealism and perfectionism. It looked at idealistic and unrealistic expectations in relationships, overly perfectionistic standards, and having the accompanying personality issues of narcissism and damaged self-esteem. The hypothesis was that these would be more likely to be characteristic of those who hadn't been able to find and sustain a marriage than those who had. This was determined in several ways: whether the participants consciously attributed these traits and ways of thinking to themselves, whether they selected the items that describe relationships that were linked with these variables, and whether they reported hearing the "messages" during their childhood that could be considered to be programming for unrealistic expectations.

HYPOTHESIS #5: Singles are more likely than marrieds to report idealistic and/or perfectionistic beliefs and behaviors.

Personality Influence – Fear of Loss

Another concept frequently proposed in the psychological literature to explain relationship difficulties is the fear of intimacy or commitment. The second personality variable considered in my study was one element of this fear that could account for ways of interacting that might result in remaining single. That fear is the threat of loss. Three possible types of this threat were differentiated. First was the fear of the loss of the other, focusing on concerns about abandonment, rejection, and disappointment. The second, fear of the loss of the self, addressed engulfment, loss of identity, and loss of control. The third was the fear of the loss of freedom, which dealt with feelings of entrapment, limiting of one's options, and the loss of choice.

These three types of fear of loss were selected as a way of clarifying some of the different possible perspectives on this issue. It wasn't presumed that all issues about loss were included or that these three are mutually exclusive of one another. Certainly there is overlap in the concepts. The study just looked at the extent to which any or all of the fears might be more likely to characterize singles when compared with married subjects.

HYPOTHESIS #6: Singles are more likely than marrieds to report fear related to abandonment (loss of the other).
HYPOTHESIS #7: Singles are more likely than marrieds to report fear related to engulfment (loss of the self).
HYPOTHESIS #8: Singles are more likely than marrieds to report fear related to limiting of options (loss of freedom).

Appendix B-4

My Research:
Results of the Hypotheses

ALTHOUGH THE FIRST TWO hypotheses did not have statistically significant results, all of the rest of the proposed issues were found to differentiate between the four groups: single women, single men, married women, and married men.

Environmental Influence – Early Family Relationships

HYPOTHESIS #1: Singles and marrieds are likely to differ in their views of their parents and/or their parents' relationship.

Consistent with much of the previous research that unsuccesfully attempted to find evidence that links parents with mate selection, this hypothesis lacked significant findings. Many theorists have proposed the link, but empirical evidence has not validated it. Although the study didn't find significant differences on perception of their parents, there was a small (but not statistically significant) tendency for singles to be more likely than marrieds to view their parents negatively.

All participant groups were more likely to rate their parents' marriage as "stable" than as "happy." Nearly half of the singles (50% of women, 46% of men) described their parental relationship as either neutral or unhappy, compared with 41% of married females and 35% of married males reporting these ratings. Over a third of single females and a fourth of single males listed one of their reasons for not being married as "Don't want to repeat parents' marriage." This shows how important the parents' relationship was to their perception of their own future relationships, even though the differences were not statistically significant between single and married subjects in their overall view of their parents' marriages.

HYPOTHESIS #2: Singles are more likely than marrieds to view their parents and/or their parents' relationship as either highly negative or as highly positive.

Differences in extremes of attitudes toward parents also failed to be validated by the data. Singles were somewhat less likely to have highly positive views of their parents or their parents' relationship and were slightly more likely to express highly negative views, but the differences were, again, not statistically significant. Whether there's any validity to the idea that extreme perceptions about parents represents unresolved separation issues, these results gave no reason to believe that singles were any more extreme than married subjects in their views. This was consistent with the list of reasons singles gave for why they hadn't yet married, since they were unlikely to select either of the items that most closely correlated with a lack of separation: "Emotional involvement with parents" and "Taking care of parent/sibling."

The only difference that was found to be significant in this part of the results was that married females were more likely than single females to give a highly positive rating of their father. This could be interpreted to mean that women who had positive paternal relationships were able to have a healthy separation and go on to form a positive marital relationship.

One interesting observation that was true for all of the groups was that the most negatively rated parental characteristics were the traditional stereotypes: the mothers were described as being "easily upset" and fathers were said to be "withdrawn" or "reserved."

HYPOTHESIS #3: Singles are more likely than marrieds to report having received messages that might characterize intimate relationships in a negative or an idealistic way.

Despite the lack of significant differences on the first two hypotheses, results from this hypothesis did support the importance of early influences on expectations in intimate relationships. Consistent with the idea that a person's perceptions of marriage are transmitted from the family of origin and that early "messages" do result in beliefs that later impact behavior, the results of the data on this hypothesis showed statistical differences between the groups. Singles were much more likely to report receiving a greater number of messages in childhood that characterized relationships in either a negative or an unrealistic way. Although these findings alone don't prove any causal relationship between receiving detrimental messages and not marrying, they offer one potential explanation related to the status of remaining single.

There were also statistical differences based on gender. Both married and single males were much less likely than their female counterparts to report that the messages on the list applied to them. Maybe the messages that boys receive are not as likely to be relationship-oriented and are more likely to be occupation-oriented, or it could be that a different list of relationship messages might be more applicable to males. Also, men might be different in the way they understand the roots of their feelings or behavior so some messages might have been transmitted but were not as consciously received by them as boys — or just didn't have enough impact on them to remember them.

There were only two messages that differentiated between the single and married men and they were contradictory. "You will be a great catch" was reported by a third of single men but only 14% of married men. However, 40% of both groups reported a very similar message: "You will make a wonderful husband." It could be interpreted that the former message might have promoted a narcissistic or idealistic way of thinking, while the latter led to a more realistic positive self-image. The only other message showing a statistical difference between the two groups was a completely contradictory one: "No one will ever put up with you." None of the married men reported hearing this, but 14% of the single men reported that they had. This is certainly a message that can sow the seeds of self-doubt.

This same contradiction was evident in the data for women. Idealism was emphasized in the items single women reported, with half saying they were told that "Someday your prince will come" (compared with only 22% of married women) and 43% saying they were told that "You will be a great catch" (compared with only 8% of married women). Perfectionistic messages were also significantly different between the groups. One-third of single women but only 5% of married women said that they were told "No one is good enough for you," and 47% of single women but only 23% of married women said that they had been cautioned "Don't settle for second best."

The contradiction was that single women were also much more likely than married women to report hearing the opposite type of messages, those which tend to promote a negative self-concept: "Women can't be trusted" (17% of single women, but only 5% of married women), "You will scare away the opposite sex if you are too _____" (55% of single women, but only 31% of married women), "No one will ever put up with you" (22% of single women, but only 9% of married women), and "Don't enjoy yourself too much" (36% of single women, but only 20% of married women).

The contradictory nature of these results is consistent with the theory that many single women might be idealistic or searching for perfection but don't really feel worthy of it. The confusion of receiving conflicting messages about how wonderful you are, or about how someone wonderful will come along, but at the same time that no one will ever want you, cannot be underestimated.

There were also other messages that showed significant differences between the single and married females. Married women reported hearing more items that were not about intimate relationships, like "Boys will be boys" or "You will hurt your mother if you do that," while single women were more likely to hear the negative relationship messages: "Don't marry someone like I did" (28% of single women, but only 12% of married women) or "Marriage is nothing but trouble" (21% of single women, but 6% of married women).

Two messages that resulted in significant differences between the sexes for both the single and married subjects support the idea that there are stereotyped differences between the sexes in relationship training: "You will scare away the opposite sex if you are too _____" (frequently reported by women), and "The opposite sex will leave you if you give them what they want" (frequently reported by men).

Environmental Influence - Traumatic Life Experiences

HYPOTHESIS #4:   Singles are more likely than marrieds to have experienced traumatic events that might negatively influence intimate relationships.

This proposal showed statistical differences for both marital status and gender, with singles being more likely than marrieds and with women being more likely than men to report traumatic events in their lives. The negative impact of trauma on intimacy has frequently been related in the research literature to sexual abuse, parental divorce and violence, and loss. These were the issues that were examined.

Sexual Abuse. In contrast to statistics that are often reported that as many as one-third of women and one-sixth of men have been sexually molested as children or adolescents, very few subjects in this study reported this trauma, and there were no differences with respect to marital status. "Incest/child sexual abuse" was reported by 5% of the single and 6% of the married women, and 7% of the single and 9% of the married women reported having been raped. Only one woman (single) said she had been sexually abused as an adult. Of the men, only one (married) reported childhood sexual abuse. It's possible that these low figures might be explained by the high level of socioeconomic and educational background of the subjects, which might account for a lower likelihood of these traumatic experiences. However, another interpretation might be that there is a strong reluctance to report, or even to remember, this trauma, and to acknowledge it as abuse, especially if it might have been a one-time occurrence. (This study was done in the 1980's when reporting this was relatively new in the culture. Even today it's still generally under-reported.) Another possibility is that people who experienced this trauma but were reluctant to admit it, might have chosen not to finish and return the questionnaire.

Parental Divorce and Violence. "Parents argued frequently" was often reported, but it only differentiated the groups slightly, mainly for men (45% of single women and 38% of married women, but 50% of single men and 32% of married men). "Family violence" was reported much less frequently and it didn't differentiate the groups (16% of both single and married women, 10% of single men and 8% of married men). One significant item for men (24% of single but only 8% of married) but not for women (16% of single and 13% of married) was "Parents divorced." Of the single men whose parents had been divorced, 10% had experienced this by age eleven and another 50% were between eleven and eighteen at the time of the occurrence. If these boys lived with their mothers, it could be interpreted that having the father absent in the home during adolescence did affect their later courtship behavior. Perhaps they had more responsibilities at home or maybe they were reluctant to make the same painful mistake that their parents made.

Loss. There were not significant differences in early loss of a parent among the groups. Although a large percentage of participants reported parental deaths, only a few were younger than twelve years old when the loss occurred (5% of single women, 2% of married women, 7% of single men, 2% of married men), and a few between the ages of twelve and nineteen (5% of single women, 3% of married women, 2% of single men, 8% of married men). Most parental losses were experienced when the subjects were adults.

Also, very few participants reported having traumatic experiences like "Death of relationship partner," or "Serious illness/accident/injury of relationship partner," or a "Broken engagement at the last minute." A much larger number reported the traumatic experience of dealing with "Abortion" (36% of single women, 27% of married women, 26% of single men, 22% of married men), but these losses didn't differentiate the groups.

However, there were losses that did statistically differentiate the groups. Singles were more likely to select "Very unhappy love affair" (52% of single women and 45% of single men, but only 25% of married women and 12% of married men). "Broken engagement" was significantly different for women (31% of single women but only 16% of married women) but not for men (12% of both single and married men). This can validate the idea that it is difficult to rebuild the willingness to trust after a bad relationship ends, and that unhappy past experiences can contaminate new ones. Or, it could represent a personality trait related to the difficulty of bouncing back after a traumatic break-up.

The findings give some support to the idea that studies of infant attachment and loss might be applicable to adults in relationships. After being abandoned by a few love-objects, a child is left with mixed emotions, continuing to yearn for love while feeling resentment for anyone who could potentially leave them abandoned again. Extrapolate this to adults and maybe some might keep getting involved in love relationships but then sabotaging them with their own fear and underlying resentment.

In spite of the frequency of single participants reporting unhappy love affairs or broken engagements, only 14% of the women and 24% of the men attributed their single status to "Unhappy previous relationship" when listing reasons for not having married. Very few accounted for remaining single by relating it to any kind of past trauma. Most just attributed it to the bad luck of not finding the "right" person. This doesn't support the idea that people use past events as a way of "self-handicapping" in order to explain some unfortunate circumstance. But that concept is based on being under pressure to "look good," while the subjects in this study, hopefully, didn't feel a need to rationalize their situation.

It's always difficult to isolate a particular event in order to consider it a cause of a particular outcome. In this case, it's not only possible to question any cause and effect link between "Very unhappy love affair" and being single, but it's also necessary to note the probability that singles are more likely to have had this experience just <u>because</u> they remained single and were therefore available to having more relationships. The question is whether this trauma increases a person's vulnerability and, therefore, susceptibility to it reoccurring, and also whether it can have an effect on someone's ability or willingness to get involved and try again. Since at least half of the single participants were admitting to having experienced various types of painful or tragic loss in their adult relationships, it does seem reasonable to conclude that this may leave a consequential, perhaps even irreparable, scar.

Personality Influence – Idealism/Perfectionism

Considering the substantial number of popular press accounts that propose the theories (although without much research) about the two personality traits selected for my investigation, idealism/perfectionism and the fear of loss, it was not surprising to find that these hypotheses were validated by the data. It is important, however, to consider again the possible explanation that the differences found on these issues were actually because singles have been in more relationships and therefore become more focused on these traits, while married participants might feel more secure and accepting since they have already been committed to someone over a period of time. Nonetheless, there are striking differences between the groups on these personality traits. It could be useful to test for these traits at an earlier age to see whether they are in any way <u>predictive</u> of not marrying, or whether they are just the <u>outcome</u> of remaining single for an extended period of time.

HYPOTHESIS #5: Singles are more likely than marrieds to report idealistic and perfectionistic beliefs.

The results clearly showed that singles <u>were</u> more likely than marrieds to report idealistic and perfectionistic beliefs about relationships and even to openly admit that they didn't want to settle for anything less than the perfect mate, even though they were also likely to be just as critical of a potential partner as they were of themselves.

The scale of idealism/perfectionism, as well as the "messages" and "reasons for not marrying" which related to this issue, actually combined three different issues into one: (1) idealism – having unrealistic expectations, (2) perfectionism – having an overly critical attitude, and (3) self-esteem – having either grandiosity or self-doubt (or both) about one's worth.

<u>Idealism</u>. Both the single women and the single men emphasized idealistic beliefs more than any of the other categories of items. They gave very high positive ratings to: "Having the right 'chemistry' is very important to me" (this

item was rated the highest by single men), "I love romance," "Finding my 'soul mate' has been important to me," and "I love being 'in love.'" Corresponding items were the most frequently selected when they gave reasons why they hadn't married: "Unrealistic expectations" (38% of women and 26% of men) as well as "Too idealistic/romantic" (36% of women and 36% of men).

One possible explanation is that many of the participants grew up in the 40's and 50's and were strongly influenced by the idealistic television shows and romantic movies during that era. This may have created unrealistic expectations that left them dissatisfied with relationships that <u>were</u> realistic and available. Another explanation is that many people who were raised in affluence learned to expect to achieve goals easily, with little frustration or disappointment, and therefore they didn't develop the tolerance needed for resolving the conflicts that always arise in close relationships. With both of these concepts, the outcome is the same: if a relationship or partner has shortcomings, it must not be the sought-after ideal. And so the search for the elusive "chemistry" or "soul mate" continues.

These interpretations still don't explain why these individuals were more affected by these influences than were their counterparts who did marry, but the results confirm that this idealistic tendency does appear much more often in the single subjects. Longitudinal research beginning in childhood would be interesting to see if this is actually a personality trait that would predict difficulty in committed relationships or whether it's a characteristic that develops later <u>because</u> of remaining single.

There are many speculations that can be made about the inclination toward being idealistic or romantic: the need to escape from what is seen as an unpleasant reality, the wish to remedy disappointing parental relationships, a way of avoiding intimacy without having to admit to doing it, or maybe a frustrated desire to simply believe in some noble principle. Maybe these singles might have been the ones, in past centuries, who would have dedicated their lives to exploring the world or fighting for causes or finding homes for orphans — and they would have been less conflicted about not getting married.

<u>Perfectionism</u>. The single women gave higher ratings to "I am my own worst critic" than to any other item on the idealism/perfectionism scale. This item was

also given very high ratings by single men, along with three others: "There aren't very many people who are my 'type,'" "I believe there are only a few people who would be right for me," and "I wonder if anyone would really be suitable for me." All of these are perfectionistic items.

The reasons given for not having married that fell into this scale of personality traits also strongly supported a perfectionistic inclination. The items most frequently chosen were: "Always find something wrong with partners" (48% of women and 55% of men), "Unable to find the right person" (83% of women and 88% of men), "Those I'm interested in aren't available/already taken" (57% of women and 50% of men), and "Not interested in those interested in me" (50% of women and 36% of men).

One interpretation of these responses is that an overly critical attitude becomes a way of escaping from feelings of fear and disappointment that many singles previously experienced with respect to intimate relationships. Perfectionism theorists say the trait develops from being raised with disapproval or inconsistent or conditional approval. To analyze this trait in early life as it relates to difficulty in adult intimacy is something that would be interesting with long-term research.

Self-Esteem. These items were less likely to be given significant ratings than the items oriented toward idealistic and perfectionistic beliefs. The only one with especially positive ratings was one that was frequently selected by single men: "I believe that I am 'special' when it comes to relationships." This may relate to unrealistic expectations due to narcissism. Generally, though, self-esteem issues were more visible in messages from childhood and in the reasons given for not having married. Three reasons for not being married that were often reported showed the frustration of the participants, which also can be seen as self-doubt: "Unable to sustain lasting relationship" (48% of women, 33% of men), "Those I'm interested in aren't interested in me" (48% of women, 48% of men), and "I'm doing something wrong" (36% of women, 26% of men). However, there were few participants who selected "Physical unattractiveness," "Social inadequacy," "Try too hard," or "Something is wrong with me" as reasons for not having married, all of which are much more closely related to having a negative self-image.

Personality Influence – Fear Of Loss

Theorists say that immature or narcissistic relationships are dominated by the attempt to compensate for unmet needs from childhood, including having excessive fears about abandonment, and also having conflict between the wish to be dependent and the desire for independence. Although these unmet needs didn't show up in responses about early family relationships, the conflicts and fears were very apparent in the items about fear of loss as well as the reasons selected for not having married. All of the scales of fear of loss showed highly significant differences based on marital status, with both female and male singles being <u>much</u> more likely than their married counterparts to express fear of loss as a concern in their relationships.

HYPOTHESIS #6: Singles are more likely than marrieds to report fear related to abandonment (loss of the other).

The validation of this hypothesis is consistent with infant attachment studies that propose that fear of being abandoned often develops into a tendency to remain distant or uncommitted in relationships. This also supports the idea that perfectionists have difficulty in relationships because they are anticipating being rejected. They fear that they can't meet up to their own standards (and so reject themselves) and they are also hypersensitive to the criticism of others, which keeps them distant and self-protective. These issues were very evident in the fear of abandonment and rejection expressed by many of the unmarried subjects, especially the women.

The biggest concern on this scale that was expressed by single men (but also by both married women and married men) was the item "Arguing or fighting makes me think the relationship is in trouble." This was followed by "I seem to need a lot of reassurance that my partner wants to be with me," and "I worry about what will happen if the relationship doesn't work out." Abandonment fears that were expressed by the single women were similar, but first came the need for reassurance, followed by concern about arguing or fighting, and then they also selected the item that overtly stated "I'm afraid of being abandoned."

These findings were even further validated by the reasons that were given for not being married, especially by the women: "Fear of abandonment" (28% of women, 12% of men), "Fear of rejection" (33% of women, 17% of men), "Don't want to risk getting hurt" (31% of women, 17% of men).

HYPOTHESIS #7: Singles are more likely than marrieds to report fear related to engulfment (loss of the self).

The potential for being overwhelmed by a relationship or a partner was clearly a concern for single subjects as compared to married subjects based on the findings for this scale. It could be that singles fear not having a distinct sense of their own personal identity, or fear not being assertive enough to maintain their individuality within a close relationship. This is consistent with theories about unresolved separation-individuation issues. Another interpretation, though, is that the fear is a result of experiencing prior relationship losses and feeling threatened by the idea of again becoming involved in still another new and unpredictable intimate situation. More than a third of the single women (but only 7% of single men) listed "Fear of dependency" as a reason for not marrying.

The two biggest concerns reported on this scale were similar for both the single women and the single men: "I'm uncomfortable letting my partner be in control" and "When someone is really interested in me, I tend to lose interest and back away." For men, these items were followed by "I feel smothered." For women, the next item most frequently selected was "I worry about losing my sense of myself as an independent person."

Two reasons reported for not having married which support fears of engulfment were: "Don't want to lose privacy" (29% of women, 14% of men), and "Like being alone" (28% of women and 19% of men).

HYPOTHESIS #8: Singles are more likely than marrieds to report fear related to limiting of options (loss of freedom).

Consistent with most stereotypic expectations of male-female behavior, women expressed more concern than men did about fear of abandonment while men attached more importance than women did to fear of the loss of freedom. The difference wasn't very substantial, but this was the only fear with a higher mean score for single men than for single women. That is, more men than women acknowledged that many of the items applied to them that were related to the fear of having their options limited. This data supports theorists that say that fear of responsibility and fear of the loss of freedom are the major roadblocks for men in their ability to make commitments.

Confirmation of this hypothesis is consistent with the "Romantic Dilemma," which says that in the effort to maintain a balance between commitment and freedom, people seek the security and companionship of a close relationship while still wanting to avoid the responsibility and obligations of it. Another explanation underlying a fear of giving up one's freedom could be that unshakable belief that there might be a better partner available out there somewhere.

The main concern reported on this scale by both the single women and men was: "I fear losing the freedom to do what I want to do when I want to do it." This apparently was not related to dating other people, because the least likely concern reported both by women and men was "It bothers me to feel that I can't date outside the relationship." The items that did follow as concerns for women were "I tend to wish I could be in two places at once" and "I feel resentful when I have to give things up for my relationship." Those that followed for men were "Making choices tends to be a painstaking process for me" and then the wish to be in two places at once.

Even more support for the significance of this fear of loss of freedom was found in the reasons that singles reported for not being married: "Fear of being 'tied down'" (24% of women, 38% of men), "Want to maintain freedom" (21% of women, 29% of men), "Unwilling to assume responsibility" (12% of women, 29% of men), and "Remaining open to new opportunities" (26% of women, 33% of men).

Reported Reasons For Not Marrying

Most of the frequently reported reasons that the single subjects gave for having remained unmarried have already been discussed in the sections above. Generally, the reasons given were consistent with having idealistic and perfectionistic beliefs as well as with all three of the different types of fear of loss that were explored. The reason that was the most frequently given by both female and male participants was simply that they were "Unable to find the right person" (83% of women and 88% of men), often romantically described as "inability to find one's 'true love.'" Some other reasons given the most frequently were: "Those I'm interested in aren't available/already taken" (57% of women, 50% of men), "Not interested in those interested in me" (50% of women, 36% of men), and "Always find something wrong with partners" (48% of women, 55% of men).

These were followed by "Unable to sustain lasting relationships" (48% of women, 33% of men), "Don't want to repeat parents' marriage" (36% of women, 26% of men), "Occupation prevents meeting people" (29% of women, 24% of men), "Remaining open to new opportunities" (26% of women, 33% of men), "Want to maintain freedom" (21% of women, 29% of men), "Unwilling to assume responsibility" (only 12% of women but 29% of men), and, the most obvious, "Fear of commitment" (24% of women, 14% of men).

APPENDIX B-5

My Research: Limitations and Conclusions

Limitations

It's always necessary to recognize some of the limitations of the study, including issues related to the demographics of the people who responded to the questionnaire, the percentage of people who completed and returned the questionnaire (the response rate), as well as some of the specific items themselves.

THE DEMOGRAPHICS

The two groups, "singles" and "marrieds," were well matched on all demographic characteristics except age and the statistical difference on this was very small (the mean age of singles was 38.7 years and the mean age of marrieds was 40.3 years). All subjects were born between 1940 and 1950 (the study was done in 1985). With respect to the idea that better educated individuals might be less likely to marry, in this study most subjects were highly educated and this was very similar across all of the groups.

The married participants were a stable population with respect to relationships, with more than 60% having been married for ten years or more and with only 14% having been married more than once. Just 2% of single participants were living with a partner at the time of the study (the requirement was that it had to be for less than a year) but 63% of them had been in a cohabiting relationship at least once in the past. Nearly one third of the single females and 12% of the single males had been engaged at least once. This indicates that these participants were highly motivated to be in close relationships, and most had previously been able to achieve some level of commitment.

There was little variability with respect to race or ethnicity. The population was almost entirely Caucasian and was also very disproportionately Jewish (42% of singles, 32.5% of marrieds). This was a result of how and where the study was advertised (see Recruitment of Participants). Since all four groups that were compared were so similar on demographics, ethnicity was not considered to be an issue for the analysis, but it is noted that different races or cultures would very likely have different perceptions and experiences with respect to the variables in the study. For example, one culture might discourage showing any emotion about a traumatic event, while another might advocate a free expression of feelings. Or one culture might be more likely to blame themselves for a problem, while another culture might blame the difficulty on something external and focus on the need to overcome obstacles in life. Variations based on geographic location, on socio-economic status, and on educational background were very limited in this study and different results might have occurred with these differing populations. However, since the groups that were being compared – singles and marrieds, males and females – were so similar to one another across all of these background measures, the results were still considered valuable.

THE RESPONSE RATE

About 525 questionnaires were distributed and only 225 were returned, which is a 43% response rate. Generally, survey research uses two or three follow-up mailings to try to get at least a 50% response rate so that there isn't what is called "response bias" (that is, perhaps those who are readily willing to participate on the first try might have a particular leaning). In this case, there was no possibility of follow-up since people who participated were either responding to an advertisement or else were randomly recruited at various meetings and events with no requirement to provide a name or address. The positive side of this limitation was that anonymity was assured, making it more likely that people could respond completely honestly. It also made it possible to invite participants from various geographic locations across the country.

The original letter of introduction said that completing the questionnaire required about an hour of time. This might have been inaccurate (many said it only took about 15 minutes) but the length may have led some potential subjects to postpone or decline to complete it. Another factor that became evident from verbal as well as written feedback from some of the subjects was the emotional difficulty involved in responding to many of the questions in the study. Although people frequently wrote comments about finding the questionnaire to be very engaging and thought-provoking, some expressed finding it disturbing, especially if it caused them to reminisce about past unpleasant experiences. This might have discouraged some participants from completing the questionnaire after they received it. Since there was complete anonymity and no way to follow up, there was also no way to encourage participants to keep trying.

THE ITEMS

The items for each different results scale from the questionnaire were tested for inter-item consistency and found to have very high reliability, so it wasn't necessary to eliminate any of the items from the data analysis. However, the subscale of idealism and perfectionism, as well as the lists of messages and traumatic events, did include factors that probably could have been broken down even further into different issues in order to provide additional informative results.

For example, the idealism and perfectionism subscale, and also the messages list, included items which could have been further separated into three specific categories: (1) idealistic or unrealistic beliefs about relationships ("Someday your prince/princess will come"), (2) perfectionistic attitudes ("No one is good enough for you"), or (3) self-concept in relationships ("No one will ever want you"). Also, the list of traumatic events included items that represented experiences that were specifically relevant to romantic relationships but it also included items that were associated with other trauma that were not about relationships. It could be that a more rigorous division of items in the scoring might have provided a more in-depth understanding of each of these distinct issues.

One other limitation was that many of the questionnaire items were asked from the perspective of being single, so perhaps the married subjects may have found these items to be less relevant since they hadn't been in relationships outside of marriage for many years. Also, it wasn't entirely clear whether the responses they gave were based exclusively on their marital relationship or were also based on prior social experiences. This inconsistency could have accounted for some of the differences between married and single responses.

THE TIMING

Last but not least, the questionnaire study was done in the 1980s and there have been many social changes since then, both in relationship expectations and in parenting techniques. Although it's possible that these issues might have less effect on the midlife people of today, it might be less different than we might think. It would be interesting to repeat the study to see if the hypothesized differences between the single and married subjects do still exist.

Conclusions

From the data collected in this study, it was reasonable to conclude that midlife singles do, in fact, differ from their married counterparts in a number of specific ways. They're more likely to report having heard negative and/or idealistic messages about relationships during their childhood. They're more likely to have experienced traumatic events that could have negatively influenced their partnerships. They're more likely to admit to having idealistic and perfectionistic beliefs about intimate relationships. And they're more likely to acknowledge having fears related to loss, including abandonment, engulfment, and the loss of freedom.

The importance of the wish for the ideal — the perfect mate — is clear, but how it develops is not. The unresolved separation-individuation explanation was not strongly supported by the data on the parental relationship, but there was evidence from other parts of the data that this concept might still play some role. Maybe these singles were more susceptible to the unrealistic expectations that they learned from romantic movies or family shows on television because of their bonding and separation issues or because of the "messages" that they heard from their parents about intimate relationships and about themselves. Or maybe they had a strong desire to believe the negative messages passed on by their families were really not true after all.

Doing long-term research starting in childhood might show whether these beliefs are learned from someone's upbringing or whether some people are just inclined toward idealistic or perfectionistic characteristics or thinking, leading them to have unrealistic expectations or thwarting their ability to establish connections in the complicated world of relationships. Or maybe these same traits might make some of these individuals more suitable for successes and accomplishments that are more difficult for their peers that are more "tied down" in their marriages.

Equity theory says that people have to feel that they have enough to offer in the "marketplace" to make a fair exchange for the partnership they are seeking. It may be that these singles didn't feel that they had sufficient assets to be worthy of a "perfect" partner, even though that is what they continued to want. And, if they are so critical of themselves, maybe they are also less capable of accepting the flaws of another enough to be able to just relax and enjoy a satisfying and fulfilling relationship.

The findings do point to a link between the hypothesized variables and remaining unmarried. Still, it's necessary to consider whether the results could also be caused by some other factor in the questionnaire procedure itself, and to recognize that this was not a truly representative sample of the single population since participants were mainly white, well educated, and disproportionately Jewish. In spite of the possible limitations, though, the data certainly appear to provide validity for the idea that those who remain single are more likely to have been socialized with negative and unrealistic messages or to have experienced traumatic events that then precipitated, or became combined with, idealistic and perfectionistic beliefs as well as fears about loss.

The profile can be drawn of someone who is idealistically searching for a perfect mate and yet fearful of abandonment, engulfment, or loss of freedom — all of which are potential risks in establishing intimate and committed relationships. The results are even strong enough to propose that they can, to some extent, be generalized to other single populations and maybe also to people who were previously married but have then been unsuccessful in further attempts to make that commitment again.

The hypotheses stated that these issues were more likely to be characteristic of people who remained single into midlife than of married people in a similar age range and of comparable background. Since traits and fears are often unconscious to individuals, this could account for those who report being interested in marrying but can't seem to achieve it or to maintain it. However, on the other hand, it could also be speculated that those people who _do_ marry and remain married might have more fears of another variety — such as isolation and emptiness — than people who remain single. Therefore they might more easily accept and commit to a partner in order to assure themselves of companionship and security.

Appendix C

Quotes and Permissions

Appleton, W. S., 1981, <u>Fathers and Daughters</u>, pp. 130-131. NY: Doubleday. Excerpt used with permission from Penguin Random House.

Bach, George R., and Ronald M. Deutsch, 1971, Pairing, pp. ix-x. NY: Avon Books. Excerpt used with permission from Penguin Random House.

Bakker, Cornelis B., and Marianne K. Bakker-Rabdau, 1973, <u>No Trespassing! Explorations in Human Territoriality</u>, p. 82. SF: Chandler and Sharp Publishers. Excerpt used with permission from the authors.

Bengis, Ingrid, 1972, <u>Combat in the Erogenous Zone</u>, pp. 13, 197-198, 203, 204-205. NY: Knopf.

Blau, Peter, 1964, Exchange and Power in Social Life, p. 227. NY: Wiley. Excerpt used with permission from Taylor and Francis Group, LLC, a division of Informa plc, through Copyright Clearance Center, Inc..

Boorstein, S., 1979, "Troubled Relationships: Transpersonal and Psychoanalytic Approaches," p. 135. <u>J. of Transpersonal Psychology,</u> 11, pp. 129-139. Excerpt used with permission from the Association for Transpersonal Psychology, Palo Alto, CA.

Bowlby, John, 1982, Attachment, (2nd ed), p. 28. NY: Basic Books. Excerpt used with permission from Perseus Domestic, Hachette Book Group.

Camus, Albert, <u>Notebooks</u>, 1942-1951, p. 235. NY: Knopf, 1965. Excerpt used with permission from Rowman and Littlefield, for Editions Gallimard 1964.

Cowan, Connell, and Melvin Kinder, 1985, <u>Smart Women, Foolish Choices</u>, pp. 5-6, 201-201, 220. NY: Crown Books. Excerpts used with permission from Penguin Random House.

Critelli, J.W., and L.R. Waid, 1980, "Physical Attractiveness, Romantic Love, and Equity Restoration in Dating Relationships," p. 625. <u>J. of Personality Assessment</u>, 44, pp. 624-649. Excerpt used with permission from Taylor and Francis, Ltd, through Copyright Clearance Center, Inc..

Erikson, Erik, 1963, <u>Childhood and Society</u>, p. 263. NY: W. W. Norton. Copyright 1950, 1963 by W. W. Norton & Co., Inc., renewed 1978, 1991 by Erik H. Erikson. Excerpt used with permission from W. W. Norton & Company, Inc..

Fasteau, Marc F., 1975, <u>The Male Machine</u>, p 72. NY: Dell. Excerpt used with permission from McGraw-Hill Education.

Freud, Sigmund, and Joseph Breuer, 1895, <u>Studies on Hysteria</u>. NY: Basic Books.

Haley, Jay, 1963, <u>Strategies of Psychotherapy</u>. NY: Grune and Stratton. Copyright renewed 1990 by Jay Haley. Excerpt used with permission from Crown House Publishing, LLC.

Hawthorne, Nathanial. 1800s.

Housman, A.E., 1896, in <u>A Shropshire Lad</u>, pp. 20-21. NY: John Lane Company.

Kiley, Dan, 1983, <u>The Peter Pan Syndrome</u>, p. 24. NY: Avon Books. Excerpt used with permission from Morhaim Literary Agency, Inc., as agent for the author.

Kubie, Lawrence S., 1956, "Psychoanalysis and marriage," p. 15, in V. W. Eisenstein (editor), <u>Neurotic Interaction in Marriage</u>, (pp. 10-43). NY: Basic Books. Excerpt used with permission from Perseus Domestic, Hachette Book Group.

Mornell, Pierre, 1979, <u>Passive Men, Wild Women</u>, pp. 119-120. NY: Random House. Excerpt used with permission from Penguin Random House.

Novak, William, 1983, <u>The Great American Man Shortage and Other Roadblocks to Romance</u>, pp. 7, 16, 94-95. NY: Rawson Associates. Excerpts used with permission from the author.

Pogo comic strip, 1970.

Pope, Kenneth S. (Editor), 1980, <u>On Love and Loving</u>. San Francisco: Jossey-Bass. Excerpt used with permission from the author.

Rubin, Lillian B, 1983, <u>Intimate Strangers</u>, pp. 4, 83, 84-85. NY: Harper & Row. Excerpts used with permission from Dunham Literary, Inc., as agent for the author.

Saint-Exupery, Antoine de, 1943, <u>The Little Prince</u>. NY: Harcourt, Brace & World. Copyright renewed in 1971 by Consuelo de Saint-Exupery. English translation copyright renewed in 2000 by Richard Howard. Excerpts used with permission from Houghton Mifflin Harcourt Publishing Company.

Smotherman, Ron, 1980, <u>Winning Through Enlightenment</u>. San Francisco: Context Publications.

Twain, Mark. 1800's.

Unknown.

Viorst, Judith, 1965, <u>The Village Square</u>, p. 17. NY: Coward-McCann. Excerpt used with permission from Susan Ramer, agent for the author, at Don Congdon Associates, Inc..

Waller, Willard, 1937, "The Rating and Dating Complex," p. 728. <u>American Sociological Review</u>, 2, pp.727-734.

Appendix D

Bibliography

Adams, G. R., and Huston, T. L. "Social Perceptions of Middle-aged Persons Varying in Physical Attractiveness." <u>Developmental Psychology</u>, 1975, 11, pp.657-658.

Anastasi, A. <u>Psychological Testing</u>. 1982, NY: Macmillan.

Appleton, W. S. <u>Fathers and Daughters</u>. 1981, NY: Doubleday.

Aron, A., et al. "Relationships with Opposite-sexed Parents and Mate Choice." <u>Human Relations</u>, 1974, 27, pp. 17-24.

Babbie, E. R. <u>The Practice of Social Research</u>. 1979, Belmont, CA: Wadsworth Publ.

Bach, George R., and Deutsch, R. M. <u>Pairing</u>. 1971, NY: Avon Books.

Bailey, R. C., and Kelly, M. "Perceived Physical Attractiveness in Early, Steady, and Engaged Daters." <u>J. of Psychology</u>, 1984, 116, pp. 39-43.

Bakos, S. C. <u>This Wasn't Supposed to Happen: Single Women Over Thirty Talk Frankly About Their Lives</u>. 1985, NY: Continuum.

Barkas, J. L. <u>Single in America</u>. 1980, NY: Atheneum.

Barnett, R. C., and Baruch, G. K. "Women in the Middle Years: A Critique of Research and Theory." Psychology of Women Quarterly, 1978, 3, pp. 87-97.

Beck, A. T. Cognitive Therapy and the Emotional Disorders. 1976, NY: International Universities Press.

Bengis, Ingrid. Combat in the Erogenous Zone. 1972, NY: Knopf.

Bergland, Christopher. "Depression and Anger Across 25 Years: Changing Vulnerabilities in the VSA model." J. of Family Psychology, 2014, 28, #2, pp. 225-235.

Bernard, J. The Future of Marriage. 1972, NY: World.

Berne, Eric. Transactional Analysis in Psychotherapy. 1961, NY: Grove Press.

Bernstein, D. M., et al. "Pursuing and Distancing: the Construct and its Management." J. of Personality Assessment, 1985, 49, pp. 273-281.

Birnbaum, J. A. "Life Patterns and Self-esteem in Gifted Family Oriented and Career Committed Women." In M. T. S. Mednick et al., Women and Achievement: Social and Motivational Analysis, 1975, Washington: Hemisphere, pp. 396-419.

Birthchnell, J. "Recent Parent Death and Mental Illness." British J. of Psychiatry, 1970, 116, pp. 289-297.

Blalock, H. M., Jr. Social Statistics. 1979, NY: McGraw-Hill.

Blau, Peter. Exchange and Power in Social Life. 1964, NY: Wiley.

Bloom, D. E., and Bennett, N. G. Marriage Patterns in the United States. 1985, Discussion Paper #85-4, Cambridge, MA: Harvard University, Center for Population Studies.

Bolles, R. C. Learning Theory. 1979, NY: Holt, Rinehart, and Winston.

Boorstein, S. "Troubled Relationships: Transpersonal and Psychoanalytic

Approaches." J. of Transpersonal Psychology, 1979, 11, pp. 129-139.

Booth, A., et al. "Impact of Parental Divorce on Courtship." J. of Marriage and the Family, 1984, 46, pp. 85-94.

Borins, E. F. M., and Forsythe, P. J. "Past Trauma and Present Functioning of Patients Attending a Women's Psychiatric Clinic." Am. J. of Psychiatry, 1985, 142, pp. 460-463.

Bowlby, John. "The Making and Breaking of Affectional Bonds: 1. Aetiology and Psychopathology in the Light of Attachment Theory." British J. of Psychiatry, 1977, 130, pp. 201-210.

Bowlby, John. Attachment. 1982, NY: Basic Books.

Brim, O. G., et al. "The MIDUS National Survey: An Overview." In How Healthy Are We? A National Study of Well-being at Midlife, 2004, Chapter One, pp. 1-36.

Brown, G. W., and Harris, T. Social Origins of Depression: A Study of Psychiatric Disorder in Women. 1978, London: Tavistock.

Brown, G. W., et al. "Depression and Loss." British J. of Psychiatry, 1977, 130, pp. 1-18.

Burgess, A. W., and Lazare, A. Community Mental Health: Target Populations. 1976, Englewood Cliffs, NJ: Prentice-Hall.

Burns, D. D. "The Perfectionist's Script for Self-Defeat." Psychology Today, November 1980, pp. 34-44.

Burns, D. D., and Beck, A. T. "Cognitive Behavior Modification of Mood Disorders." In J. P. Foreyt and D. P. Rathjen (Eds), Cognitive Behavior Therapy: Research and Application, 1978, NY: Plenum, pp. 109-134.

Campbell, A. "The American Way of Mating." Psychology Today, May 1975, pp. 37-43.

Campbell, A., et al. The Quality of American Life: Perceptions, Evaluations, and Satisfactions. 1976, NY: Russell Sage Foundation.

Cargan, L. "Singles: An Examination of Two Stereotypes." Family Relations, 1981, 30, pp. 377-385.

Chinen, Allan B. Once Upon a Midlife: Classic Stories and Mythic Tales to Illuminate the Middle Years. 1993, NY: Tarcher Books.

Clayton, R. R., and Voss, H. L. "Shacking Up: Cohabitation in the 1970's." J. of Marriage and the Family, 1977, 39, pp. 273-283.

Clingman, J. M. "Double Standard of Age." J. of Psychology, 1983, 115, pp. 281-290.

Cohen, J. A. "Theories of Narcissism and Trauma." American J. of Psychotherapy, 1981, 35, pp. 93-100.

Cooper, C. L. "Cumulative Trauma and Stress at Work." Accounting, Organizations and Society, 1980, 5, pp. 357-359.

Costello, C. G. "Loss as a Source of Stress in Psychopathology." In R. W. J. Neufeld (Ed), Psychological Stress and Psychopathology, 1982, NY: McGraw-Hill, pp. 93-124.

Cowan, C., and Kinder, M. Smart Women, Foolish Choices. 1985, NY: Crown Books.

Cowan, G., et al. "Effects of Target, Age, and Gender on Use of Power Strategies." J. of Personality and Social Psychology, 1984, 47, pp. 1391-1398.

Critelli, J. W., and Baldwin, A. C. "Birth Order: Complementarity vs. Homogamy as Determinants of Attraction in Dating Relationships." Perceptual and Motor Skills, 1979, 49, pp. 467-471.

Critelli, J. W., and Waid, L. R. "Physical Attractiveness, Romantic Love, and Equity Restoration in Dating Relationships." J. of Personality Assessment, 1980, 44, pp. 624-649.

DeGree, C. E., and Snyder, C. R.   "Adler's Psycholgy (of Use) Today: Personal History of Traumatic Life Events as a Self-Handicapping Strategy." J. of Personality and Social Psychology, 1985, 48, pp. 1512-1519.

DeYoung, M.   The Sexual Victimization of Children. 1982, Jefferson, NC. McFarland.

Dion, K. K., and Dion, K. L.   "Self-esteem and Romantic Love."   J. of Personality, 1975, 43, pp. 39-57.

Dohrenwend, B. P., and Dohrenwend, B. S.   Stressful Life Events: Their Nature and Effects. 1974, NY: Wiley.

Dohrenwend, B. S., et al.   "Symptoms, Hassles, Social Supports, and Life Events: Problem of Confounded Measures." J. of Abnormal Psychology, 1984, 93, pp. 222-230.

Donaldson, M. A., and Gardner, R., Jr.   "Diagnoses and Treatment of Traumatic Stress Among Women After Childhood Incest."   In C. R. Figley (Ed), Trauma and Its Wake: The Study and Treatment of Post-traumatic Stress Disorder, 1985, NY: Brunner/Mazel, pp. 356-377.

Driscoll, R., et al.   "Parental Interference and Romantic Love: The Romeo and Juliet Effect." J. of Personality and Social Psychology, 1972, 24, pp. 1-10.

Durham, Jeff.   "Still Single in Midlife."   www.AMidlifeCrisis.co.uk, October 8, 2012.

Eckland, B. K.   "Theories of Mate Selection."   Social Biology, 1982, 29, pp. 7-21.

Engel, Lewis, and Ferguson, T.   "When Parents Send Bad Messages."   Medical Self-Care Magazine, 1985, September, pp. 32-36.

Erdwins, C. J., and Mellinger, J. C.   "Mid-life Women: Relation of Age and Role to Personality." J. of Personality and Social Psychology, 1984, 47, pp. 390-395.

Erickson, Milton H.   "Hypnotic Investigation of Psychodynamic Processes."   In E. L. Rossi (Ed), The Collected Papers of Milton H. Erickson on Hypnosis, Vol. III, 1980, NY: Irvington.

Erikson, Eric. Childhood and Society. 1963, NY: W. W. Norton.

Falbo, T., and Peplau, L. A. "Power Strategies in Intimate Relationships." J. of Personality and Social Psychology, 1980, 38, pp. 618-628.

Fasteau, M. F. The Male Machine. 1975, NY: Dell.

Feingold, A. "Do Taller Men Have Prettier Girlfriends?" Psychological Reports, 1982, 50, p. 810.

Figley, C. R. Stress Disorders Among Vietnam Veterans. 1978, NY: Brunner/Mazel.

Fine, M., and Hovestadt, A. J. "Perceptions of Marriage and Rationality by Levels of Perceived Health in the Family of Origin." J. of Marital and Family Therapy, 1984, 10, pp. 193-195.

Finkelhor, D., and Brown, A. "The Traumatic Impact of Child Sexual Abuse: A Conceptualization." American J. of Orthopsychiatry, 1985, 55, pp. 530-541.

Fitzpatrick, Jacki, Elizabeth Sharp, and Alan Reifman. "Midlife Singles' Willingness to Date Partners with Heterogeneous Characteristics." Family Relations, February 2009, 58, #1, pp. 121-133.

Folkes, V. S. "Forming Relationships and the Matching Hypotheses." Personality and Social Psychology Bulletin, 1982, 8, pp. 631-636.

Forsstrom-Cohen, B., and Rosenbaum, A. "Effects of Parental Marital Violence on Young Adults: An Exploratory Investigation." J. of Marriage and the Family, 1985, 47, pp. 467-472.

Freud, Sigmund. Basic Writings of Sigmund Freud, 1938, NY: Random House.

Freud, Sigmund. "Moses and Monotheism." In J. Strachey (Ed), The Standard Edition of the Complete Psychological Works of Sigmund Freud, 1964, London: Hogarth Press, Vol. 23, pp. 1-207 (original work 1939).

Freud, Sigmund, and Breuer, Josef. "Studies on Hysteria." In J. Strachey (Ed), The

Standard Edition of the Complete Psychological Works of Sigmund Freud, 1964, London: Hogarth Press, Vol. 2 (original work 1895).

Friedman, R., and Cohen, K. "The Peer-support Group: A Model for Dealing with the Emotional Aspects of Miscarriage." Group, 1980, 4, pp. 42-48.

Fromm, Eric. The Art of Loving, 1956, NY: Harper and Row.

Furst, S. (Ed). Psychic Trauma, 1967, NY: Basic Books.

"Games Singles Play." Newsweek, 1973, July 16, pp. 52-58.

Glenn, N. D., and Weaver, C. N. "The Contribution of Marital Happiness to Global Happiness." J. of Marriage and the Family, 1981, 43, pp. 161-168.

Goldberg, A. "On the Incapacity to Love." Archives of General Psychiatry, 1972, 26, pp. 3-7.

Goldberg, H. The Hazards of Being Male, 1977, NY: New American Library.

Goldberg, M. "Dynamics of Marital Interaction and Marital Conflict." Psychiatric Clinics of North America, 1982, 5, pp. 449-467.

Gordon, M. "Was Waller Ever Right? The Rating and Dating Complex Reconsidered." J. of Marriage and the Family, 1981, 43, pp. 67-76.

Gormally, J., et al. "Relationship Between Maladaptive Cognitions and Social Anxiety." J. of Consulting and Clinical Psychology, 1981, 49, pp. 300-301.

Gough, H. G., and Heilbrun, A. B. The Adjective Check List Manual, 1965, Palo Alto, CA: Consulting Psychologists Press.

Gurin, E., et al. Americans View Their Mental Health, 1960, NY: Basic Books.

Gurman, A. S., and Kniskern, D. P. "Research on Marital and Family Therapy: Progress, Perspective, and Prospect." In S. L. Garfield and A. E. Bergin (Eds), Handbook of Psychotherapy and Behavior Change: An Empirical Analysis, 1978,

NY: Wiley, pp. 817-901.

Hakansson, Krister, et al. "Association Between Mid-Life Marital Status and Cognitive Function in Later Life: Population Based Cohort Study" (Sweden). British Medical Journal (BMJ), July 2, 2009.

Haley, Jay. Strategies of Psychotherapy, 1963, NY: Grune and Stratton.

Hamachek, D. E. "Psychodynamics of Normal and Neurotic Perfectionism." Psychology, 1978, 15, pp. 27-33.

Hartnett, J., and Elder, D. "The Princess and the Nice Frog: Study in Person Perception." Perceptual and Motor Skills, 1973, 37, pp. 863-866.

Heiger, L. J., and Troll, L. "A 3-generation Study of Attitudes Concerning the Importance of Romantic Love in Mate Selection." Gerontologist, 1975, 13, p. 86.

Herman, J. L., and Hirschmann, L. Father-daughter Incest. 1981, Cambridge, MA: Harvard University Press.

Hill, C. T., et al. "Breakups Before Marriage: The End of 103 Affairs." J. of Social Issues, 1976, 32 (1), pp. 147-168.

Holahan, C. K. "Marital Attitudes Over 40 Years: A Longitudinal and Cohort Analysis." J. of Gerontology, 1984, 39, pp. 49-57.

Holmes, T. H., and Rahe, R. H. "The Social Readjustment Rating Scale." J. of Psychosomatic Research, 1967, 11, pp. 213-218.

Horney, Karen. Our Inner Conflicts. 1945, NY: W. W. Norton.

Horney, Karen. Neurosis and Human Growth: The Struggle Toward Self-realization. 1950, NY: W. W. Norton.

Horowitz, M. J. Stress Response Syndromes. 1976, NY: Jason Aronson.

Horowitz, M. J. "Disasters and Psychological Responses to Stress." Psychiatric

Annals, 1985, 15 (3), pp. 161-167.

Howell, D. C. Statistical Methods for Psychology. 1982, Boston: Duxbury Press. Humphries, Courtney. "Data Mining the Heart: How Do We Choose a Mate? What Scientists are Learning from Online Dating. A Flood of New Information is Starting to Yield the Answers." Boston Globe, 22 August 2010, Column 1.

Huston, T., and Levinger, G. "Interpersonal Attraction and Relationships." Annual Review of Psychology, 1978, 29, pp. 115-156.

Institute for Personality and Ability Testing, Inc. "16PF." 1978, Champaign, IL: Author.

Jacques, Elliot. "Death and the Midlife Crisis." International J. of Psychoanalysis, 1965.

Jason, L. A., et al. "Characteristics of Significant Dating Relationships: Male vs. Female Initiators, Idealized vs. Actual Settings." J. of Psychology, 1981, 109, pp. 185-190.

Jedlicka, D. "Sex Inequality, Aging and Innovation in Preferential Mate Selection." The Family Coordinator, 1978, 27, pp. 137-140.

Jedlicka, D. "Formal Mate Selection Networks in the U.S." Family Relations, 1980, 29, pp. 199-203.

Jedlicka, D. "Indirect Parental Influence on Mate Choice: A Test of the Psychoanalytic Theory." J. of Marriage and the Family, 1984, 46, pp. 65-70.

Jones, R. M, and Adams, G. R. "Assessing the Importance of Physical Attractiveness Across the Life-Span." J. of Social Psychology, 1982, 118, pp. 131-132.

Kacerguis, M. A., and Adams, G. R. "Erikson Stage Resolution: The Relationship Between Identity and Intimacy." J. of Youth and Adolescence, 1980, 9, pp. 117-126.

Kalter, N. "Children of Divorce in an Outpatient Psychiatric Population." American J. of Orthopsychiatry, 1977, 47, pp. 40-51.

Kelly, J. B., and Wallerstein, J. S. "The Effects of Parental Divorce: Experiences of the Child in Early Latency." American J. of Orthopsychiatry, 1976, 46, pp. 20-32.

Kenrick, D. T., and Gutierres, S. E. "Contrast Effects and Judgments of Physical Attraction: When Beauty Becomes a Social Problem." J. of Personality and Social Psychology, 1980, 38, pp. 131-140.

Kerckhoff, A. C., and Davis, K. "Value Consensus and Need Complementarity in Mate Selection." American Sociological Review, 1962, 27, pp. 295-303.

Kernberg, O. "Structural Derivatives of Object Relationships." International J. of Psychoanalysis, 1966, 47, p. 236.

Kiley, Dan. The Peter Pan Syndrome. 1983, NY: Avon Books.

Knox, D., and Wilson, K. "Dating Problems of University Students." College Student J., 1983, 17, pp. 225-228.

Kolevson, M. S., and Sheridan, M. J. "Tinker Bell Where Are You? A Closer Look at Father-daughter Relationships." Paper presented at the conference of the American Association of Marriage and Family Therapy, October 1984, San Francisco.

Korman, S. K. "Nontraditional Dating Behavior: Date-initiation and Date Expense — Sharing Among Feminists and Nonfeminists." Family Relations: J. of Applied Family and Child Studies, 1983, 32, pp. 575-581.

Kubie, L. S. "Psychoanalysis and Marriage: Practical and Theoretical Issues." In V. W. Eisenstein (Ed), Neurotic Interaction in Marriage, 1956, NY: Basic Books, pp. 10-43.

Kuhn, M. "How Mates Are Sorted." In H. Becker and R. Hill (Eds), Family, Marriage, and Parenthood, 1955, Boston: D. C. Health, pp. 246-275.

Kulka, R. A., and Weingarten, H. "The Long-term Effects of Parental Divorce in Childhood on Adult Adjustment." J. of Social Issues, 1979, 35 (4), pp. 50-78.

L'Abate, L. and Samples, G. T. "Intimacy Letters — Invariable Prescription for

Closeness-avoidant Couples." Family Therapy, 1983, 10, pp. 37-45.

Laplanche, J., and Pontalis, J. B.   The Language of Psycholanalysis.   1974, NY: Norton.

Larzelere, R. E., and Huston, T. L.   "The Dyadic Trust Scale: Toward Understanding Interpersonal Trust in Close Relationships." J. of Marriage and the Family, 1980, 42, pp. 595-604.

Lesnik-Oberstein, M., and Cohen, L.   "Cognitive Style, Sensation-seeking, and Assortative Mating." J. of Personality and Social Psychology, 1984, 46, pp. 112-117.

Levinger, G., and Raush, H. L. (Eds).   Close Relationships.   1977, Amherst, MA: University of Massachusetts Press.

Levinson, Daniel J.   The Seasons of a Man's Life.   1979, NY: Ballantine Books.

Levitz-Jones, E. M., and Orlofsky, J. L.   "Separation-individuation and Intimacy Capacity in College Women." J. of Personality and Social Psychology, 1985, 49, pp. 156-169.

Lewis, Karen Gail, and Sidney Moon.   "Always Single and Single Again Women: A Qualitative Study." Journal of Marital and Family Therapy, April 1997, Vol. 23, No. 2, pp. 115-134.

Lin, I-Fen, and Susan Brown.   "Unmarried Boomers Confront Old Age: A National Portrait." The Gerontologist, April 2012, 52 (2), pp. 153-165.

Linton, R.   The Study of Man.   1936, NY: Appleton-Century.

Lister, E. D.   "Forced Silence: A Neglected Dimension of Trauma." American J. of Psychiatry, 1982, 139, pp. 872-876.

Long, B. H.   "Evaluations and Intentions Concerning Marriage Among Unmarried Female Undergraduates." J. of Social Psychology, 1983, 119, pp. 235-242.

Lowenstein, S. F., et al. "A Study of Satisfactions and Stresses of Single Women in Midlife." Sex Roles, 1981, 7, pp. 1127-1141.

Lowenthal, M. F., Berkman, P. L., and Associates. Aging and Mental Disorder in San Francisco: A Social Psychiatric Study. 1967, San Francisco: Jossey-Bass.

Lowenthal, M. F., and Haven, C. "Interaction and Adaptation: Intimacy as a Critical Variable." American Sociological Review, 1968, 33, pp. 20-30.

Lowenthal, M. F., et al. Four Stages of Life: A Comparative Study of Women and Men Facing Transitions. 1975, San Francisco: Jossey-Bass.

Lowenthal, M. F., and Weiss, L. "Intimacy and Crises in Adulthood." The Counseling Psychologist, 1976, 6 (1), pp. 10-15.

Marks, Nadine. "Flying Solo at Midlife: Gender, Marital Status, and Psychological Well-Being." J. of Marriage and the Family, November 1996, 58 (4), pp. 917-932.

Mathes, E. W., and Severa, N. "Jealousy, Romantic Love, and Liking: Theoretical Considerations and Preliminary Scale Development." Psychological Reports, 1981, 49, pp. 23-31.

Mathes, E. W., and Wise, P. S. "Romantic Love and the Ravages of Time." Psychological Reports, 1983, 53, pp. 839-846.

May, Rollo. Love and Will. 1969, NY: W. W. Norton.

McAdams, D. P., and Vaillant, G. E. "Intimacy Motivations and Psychosocial Adjustment: A Longitudinal Study." J. of Personality Assessment, 1982, 46, pp. 586-593.

McDonald, J. Rape: Offenders and Their Victims. 1979, Springfield, IL: Charles C. Thomas.

Meiners, M. L., and Sheposh, J. P. "Beauty or Brains: Which Image for your Mate?" Personality and Social Psychology Bulletin, 1977, 3, pp. 262-265.

Mestrovik, S. G. "A Sociological Conceptualization of Trauma." Social Science and Medicine, 1985, 21, pp. 835-848.

Montenegro, Zenia P. "Lifestyles, Dating and Romance: A Study of Midlife Singles." An executive summary (based on MIDUS) for AARP, The Magazine, September 2003.

Moore, Monica. "Human Non-verbal Courtship Behavior — A Brief Historical Review." J. of Sex Research, 2010, 47 (2-3), pp. 171-180.

Mornell, Pierre. Passive Men, Wild Women. 1979, NY: Random House.

Murstein, B. I. "Stimulus-value-role: A Theory of Marital Choice." J. of Marriage and the Family, 1970, 32, pp. 465-481.

Murstein, B. I. (Ed) Theories of Attraction and Love. 1971, NY: Springer.

Murstein, B. I. Who Will Marry Whom? Theories and Research in Marital Choice. 1976, NY: Springer.

Murstein, B. I. "Mate Selection in the 1970's." J. of Marriage and the Family, 1980, 42, pp. 777-792.

Myers, J. K., et al. "Life Events and Psychiatric Impairment." J. of Nervous and Mental Disease, 1971, 152, pp. 149-157.

Myers, J. K., et al. "Life Events and Mental Status: A Longitudinal Study." J. of Health and Social Behavior, 1972, 13, pp. 398-406.

Nadelson, C. C., and Notman, M. T. "To Marry or Not to Marry: A Choice." American J. of Psychiatry, 1981, 138, pp. 1352-1356.

Novak, William. The Great American Man Shortage. 1983, NY: Rawson Associates.

Pacht, A. R. "Reflections on Perfection." American Psychologist, 1984, 39, pp. 386-390.

Parker-Pope, Tara. "The Midlife Crisis Goes Global." NY Times, January 30, 2008.

Parson, E. R.   "Ethnicity and Traumatic Stress: The Intersecting Point in Psychotherapy." In C. R. Figley (Ed), <u>Trauma and Its Wake: The Study and Treatment of Post-traumatic Stress Disorder</u>, 1985, NY: Brunner/Mazel, pp. 314-337.

Paterson, C. E., and Pettijohn, T. F. "Age and Human Mate Selection." <u>Psychological Reports</u>, 1982, 51, p. 70.

Paul, Elizabeth L.   "A Longitudinal Analysis of Midlife Interpersonal Relationships and Well-Being." In Margie E. Lachman and Jacquelyn Boone James (Eds), <u>Multiple Paths of Midlife Development</u>, 1997, University of Chicago Press, pp. 171-206.

Paykel, E. S., et al.   "Life Events and Depression: A Controlled Study." <u>Archives of General Psychiatry</u>, 1969, 21, pp. 753-760.

Pederson, Nancy L., Erica Spotts, and Kenji Kato.   "Genetic Influences on Midlife Functioning." In Willis (Ed) <u>Early Life Influences on Middle Age</u>, March 24, 2005, Sage Publications, pp. 65-98.

Peplau, L. A.   "Power in Dating Relationships." In J. Freeman (Ed), <u>Women: A Feminist Perspective</u>, 1979, Palo Alto: Maryfield, pp. 106-121.

Peterson, N.   <u>Our Lives for Ourselves: Women Who Have Never Married</u>. 1981, NY: G. P. Putnam's Sons.

Plaut, Victoria C., Hazel Rose Markus, and Margie E. Lachman.   "Place Matters: Consensual Features and Regional Variation in American Well-Being and Self." <u>J. of Personality and Social Psychology</u>, 2002, 83 (1), pp. 160-184.
Pope, K. S. (Ed).   <u>On Love and Loving</u>. 1980, San Francisco: Jossey-Bass.

Prince, A. J., and Baggaley, A. R. "Personality Variables and the Ideal Mate." <u>Family Life Coordinator</u>, 1963, 12, pp. 93-96.

Pynoos, R. S., and Eth, S.   "Developmental Perspective on Psychic Trauma in Childhood." In C. R. Figley (Ed), <u>Trauma and Its Wake: The Study and Treatment of Post-traumatic Stress Disorder</u>. 1985, NY: Brunner/Mazel, pp. 36-52.

Quarantelli, E. L.   "An Assessment of Conflicting Views on Mental Health: The

Consequences of Traumatic Events." In C. R. Figley (Ed), Trauma and Its Wake: The Study and Treatment of Post-traumatic Stress Disorder. 1985, NY: Brunner/Mazel, pp. 173-215.

Rempel, J. K., et al. "Trust in Close Relationships." J. of Personality and Social Psychology, 1985, 49, pp. 95-112.

Rubenstein, C. "Modern Art of Courtly Love." Psychology Today, July 1983, pp. 40-49.

Rubin, L. B. Intimate Strangers. 1983, NY: Harper & Row.

Rubin, Z. "Measurement of Romantic Love." J. of Personality and Social Psychology, 1970, 16, pp. 265-273.

Rudnitsky, H., and Warsh, D. "Cumulative Trauma." Forbes, December 1976, pp. 33-34.

Rusbult, C. E. "Commitment and Satisfaction in Romantic Associations: A Test of the Investment Model." J. of Experimental Social Psychology, 1980, 16, pp. 172-186.

Rusbult, C. E. "A Longitudinal Test of the Investment Model: The Development (and Deterioration) of Satisfaction and Commitment in Heterosexual Involvements." J. of Personality and Social Psychology, 1983, 45, pp. 101-117.

Rutter, M. Children of Sick Parents: An Environmental and Psychiatric Study. 1966, London: Oxford University Press.

Rutter, M. Maternal Deprivation Reassessed. 1972, Harmondsworth, England: Penguin Books.

Ryder, R. G., et al. "Separating and Joining Influences in Courtship and Early Marriage." American J. of Orthopsychiatry, 1971, 41, pp. 450-464.

Ryff, C. D., and Migdal, S. "Intimacy and Generativity: Self-perceived Transitions." Signs, 1984, 9, pp. 470-481.

Safilios-Rothschild, C. "Toward a Social Psychology of Relationships." Psychology of Women Quarterly, 1981, 5, pp. 377-384.

Salholz, E., et al. "Too Late for Prince Charming." Newsweek, June 2, 1986, pp. 54-61.

Sandfield, A. "Accounting for Single Status: Heterosexism and Ageism in Heterosexual Women's Talk About Marriage." Feminism and Psychology: An International J., November 2003, 13 (4), pp. 475-488.

Sassler, Sharon. "Partnering Across the Life Course: Sex, Relationships, and Mate Selection." J. of Marriage and the Family, June 2010, 72 (3), pp. 557-575.

Schaefer, M. T., and Olson, D. H. "Assessing Intimacy: The PAIR Inventory." J. of Marital and Family Therapy, 1981, 7, pp. 47-60.

Schwartz, P., and Lever, J. "Fear and Loathing at a College Mixer." Urban Life, 1976, 4, pp. 413-431.

Sears, P. S., and Barbee, A. H. "Career and Life Satisfaction Among Terman's Gifted Women." In J. Stanley et al (Eds), The Gifted and the Creative: Fifty-year Perspective, 1977, Baltimore: Johns Hopkins University Press, pp. 28-65.

Selye, H. The Stress of Life. 1978, NY: McGraw-Hill.

Shapiro, J., and Shapiro, D., Jr. "Self-Control and Relationship: Toward a Model of Interpersonal Health." J. of Humanistic Psychology, 1984, 24, pp. 91-116.

Sharp, Elizabeth, and Lawrence Ganong. "I'm a Loser, I'm Not Married, Let's Just All Look at Me: Ever-Single Women's Perception of Their Social Environment." J. of Family Issues, July 2011, 32 (7), pp. 956-980.

Sheehy, Gail. Passages: Predictable Crises of Adult Life. 1976, NY: Bantam Books.

Shulman, N. "Life Cycle Variation in Patterns of Close Relationships." J. of Marriage and the Family, 1975, 37, pp. 813-821.

Simon, R. J., et al. "The Woman PhD: A Recent Profile." In M. T. S. Mednick, et al

(Eds), <u>Women and Achievement: Social and Motivational Analyses</u>, 1975, NY: Wiley & Sons, pp. 355-371.

Sorotzkin, B. "The Quest for Perfection: Avoiding Guilt or Avoiding Shame?" <u>Psychotherapy</u>, 1985, 22, pp. 564-571.

Spanier, G. B, and Lewis, R. A. "Marital Quality: A Review of the Seventies." <u>J. of Marriage and the Family</u>, 1980, 42, pp. 825-839.

Stein, P. J. <u>Single</u>. 1976, Englewood Cliffs, NJ: Prentice-Hall.

Stewart, A. J. and Rubin, Z. "The Power Motive in the Dating Couple." <u>J. of Personality and Social Psychology</u>, 1976, 34, pp. 305-309.

Stuart, I. R., and Abt, L. E. (Eds). <u>Children of Separation and Divorce</u>. 1972, NY: Grossman.

Sullaway, M., and Christensen, A. "Assessment of Dysfunctional Interaction Patterns in Couples." <u>J. of Marriage and the Family</u>, 1983, 45, pp. 653-660.

Terman, L. M., and Oden, M. H. "Terman Study of the Gifted." In <u>The Gifted Child Grows Up: Genetic Studies of Genius, Volume 4</u>. 1947, Stanford: Stanford University Press.

Toman, W. "The Duplication Theorem of Social Relationships as Tested in the General Population." <u>Psychological Review</u>, 1971, 78, pp. 380-390.

Tomasson, R. E. "A Lower Divorce Rate is Reported." <u>The New York Times,</u> January 9, 1985, pp. C8.

Toomin, M. K. "The Child of Divorce." In R. E. Hardy and J. G. Cull (Eds), <u>Therapeutic Needs of the Family: Problems, Descriptions, and Therapeutic Approaches</u>. 1974, Springfield, IL: Charles Thomas.

Toufexis, Anastasia. "When the Ring Doesn't Fit." <u>Psychology Today</u>, November-December 1996, 29 (6), pp. 52-55.

Trimble, M. R. Post-traumatic Neurosis. 1981, Chichester, England: Wiley & Sons.

Waller, W. "The Rating and Dating Complex." American Sociological Review, 1937, 2, pp. 727-734.

Wallerstein, J. S., and Kelly, J. B. "The Effects of Parental Divorce: Experiences of the Preschool Child." J. of the American Academy of Child Psychiatry, 1975, 14, pp. 600-616.

Wallerstein, J. S., and Kelly, J. B. Surviving the Breakup: How Children and Parents Cope with Divorce. 1980, NY: Basic Books.

Whitbourne, Susan Krauss. "The Top 10 Myths about the Midlife Crisis." Psychology Today, July 21, 2012.

White, G. L. "Physical Attractiveness and Courtship Progress." J. of Personality and Social Psychology, 1980, 39, pp. 660-668.

White, S. G., and Hatcher, C. "Couple Complementarity and Similarity: A Review of the Literature." American J. of Family Therapy, 1984, 12, pp. 15-25.

Winch, R. F. "The Relation Between the Loss of a Parent and Progress in Courtship." J. of Social Psychology, 1949, 29, pp. 51-56.

Winch, R. F., et al. "The Theory of Complementary Needs in Mate Selection: An Analytic and Descriptive Study." American Sociological Review, 1954, 19, pp. 241-249.

Wolk, R. "Group Psychotherapy Process in the Treatment of Hostages Taken in Prison." Group, 1981, 5, pp. 31-36.

Yeh, Hsiu-Chen, et al. "Relationships Among Sexual Satisfaction, Marital Quality, and Marital Instability at Midlife." J. of Family Psychology, 2006, 20 (2), pp. 339-343.

ABOUT THE AUTHOR

Dr. Marilyn Cohen has a BS degree from Simmons College, Boston; an MSW from the University of Washington, Seattle; and a PhD from California School of Professional Psychology, Berkeley. She has provided psychotherapy and training for individuals and couples, as well as staff development training and organizational consultation for legal, medical, and academic professionals; public safety personnel (police, corrections, 911 dispatchers, firefighters, paramedics); and other public agencies and private industry.

She also worked for the American Psychological Association, the Stanford University Psychiatry Department, the University of Washington Psychiatry Department, and the University of California San Francisco Medical Center.

Dr. Cohen has retired from her private practice in San Francisco, Sausalito, and Palo Alto, California, and is now living in Boca Raton, Florida.